Pour Me Another: 105 Guinness Recipes

De Italian Flavors

Contents

4

INTRODUCTION

Welcome to "Pour Me Another: 105 Guinness Recipes", your ultimate guide to creating delicious dishes using one of the world's most beloved beers.

From the classics to modern takes on old favorites, this cookbook is sure to provide the perfect dish for any occasion. Whether you're a beer lover looking for a new twist on classic dishes or someone looking to expand their culinary abilities, you will find countless options to choose from.

This cookbook is all about Guinness, the beloved Irish beer that dates back to 1759 and is known for its distinctive dark flavor and creamy texture. It is appreciated by many different beer lovers around the world and its sweet, dark and smoky nuances set it apart from any other beer.

In "Pour Me Another: 105 Guinness Recipes" you'll find 105 tasty and creative recipes that will help you make the most out of this amazing beer. You'll find recipes that range from snacks and appetizers to main dishes and desserts, and even some drinks to create the perfect pairing.

These recipes allow you to get creative with Guinness in the kitchen. Learn how to make traditional dishes, like Shepherd's Pie, with a Guinness twist, or try more daring combinations like Oysters with Guinness Mignonette.

Once you start cooking with Guinness, you won't want to stop. With so many recipes to choose from, you're sure to find lots of ideas that will satisfy your beer-loving taste buds. This cookbook will provide you with the direction, the inspiration, and the tools to make a variety of scrumptious dishes that will please your palate and dazzle your guests.

Grab your pan and a bottle of Guinness and dive into the world of tasty dishes with "Pour Me Another: 105 Guinness Recipes". Everyone loves Guinness, and anyone can enjoy these delicious dishes, from amateur cooks to expert chefs.

Grab your ingredients and have fun in the kitchen with this amazing cookbook. Enjoy these 105 delicious recipes and pour yourself another!

1. Guinness Beef Stew

Guinness beef stew is a hearty Irish stew made with beef, Guinness, and vegetables. It's a one-pot meal perfect for chilly evenings!
Serving: 6
Preparation time: 30 minutes
Ready time: 2-3 hours

Ingredients:
• 2 tablespoons vegetable oil
• 2 pounds beef stew meat, cubed
• 2 tablespoons all-purpose flour
• 1 large onion, diced
• 2 cloves garlic, minced
• 2 tablespoons tomato paste
• 2 tablespoons brown sugar
• 2 tablespoons Worcestershire sauce
• 2 teaspoon thyme
• 1/2 teaspoon marjoram
• 1/2 teaspoon black pepper
• 1 teaspoon salt
• 2 cups beef broth
• 2 cups Guinness Stout
• 2 large potatoes, peeled and cubed
• 2 large carrots, peeled and sliced
• 2 celery stalks, sliced
• 2 tablespoons parsley, chopped

Instructions:
1. Heat the oil in a large pot over high heat. Brown the beef for about 5 minutes.
2. Add the flour and stir for 1 minute.
3. Add the onion, garlic, tomato paste, brown sugar, Worcestershire sauce, thyme, marjoram, pepper, and salt. Cook for 5 minutes, stirring occasionally.
4. Add the beef broth, Guinness, potatoes, carrots, and celery. Stir to combine and bring the mixture to a boil.

5. Reduce the heat to low and simmer for 2 to 3 hours, stirring occasionally.
6. Serve the stew hot, garnished with parsley.

Nutrition information:
Serving size: 1 bowl
Calories: 412
Fat: 12.9 g
Carbohydrates: 35.2 g
Protein: 32.2 g

2. Guinness Shepherd's Pie

Guinness Shepherd's Pie is a savory Irish dish made with ground beef and vegetables simmered in a creamy Guinness gravy and topped with whipped potatoes for a comforting and delicious meal.
Serving: 8
Preparation Time: 15 minutes
Ready Time: 1 hour

Ingredients:
-2 tablespoons olive oil
-2 cloves garlic, minced
-1 onion, diced
-1 lb ground beef
-1 (14.9-ounce) bottle Guinness
-1/2 cup beef stock
-2 tablespoons tomato paste
-2 tablespoons Worcestershire sauce
-1 teaspoon mustard powder
-1 teaspoon sweet paprika
-1/2 teaspoon salt
-Black pepper, to taste
-2 carrots, diced
-2 celery stalks, diced
-1 (14.5-ounce) can diced tomatoes
-2 teaspoons cornstarch
-2 tablespoons cold water

-3 large potatoes, peeled and diced
-1/2 cup milk
-2 tablespoons butter
-1/3 cup fresh parsley, chopped

Instructions:
1. Heat the oil in a large skillet over medium heat. Add the garlic and onion and cook until softened, about 3 minutes.
2. Add the ground beef and cook until it is no longer pink, about 5 minutes.
3.Add the Guinness, beef stock, tomato paste, Worcestershire sauce, mustard powder, paprika, salt, and pepper. Stir to combine.
4. Add the carrots, celery, and tomatoes and stir. Simmer for 15 minutes or until the vegetables are tender.
5. In a small bowl, stir together the cornstarch and water until smooth. Add to the skillet and stir into the mixture until it thickens.
6. Preheat the oven to 375°F.
7. Place the potatoes in a large pot and cover with cold water. Bring to a boil and cook until the potatoes are tender, about 15 minutes.
8. Drain the potatoes and return them to the pot. Add the milk, butter, and parsley. Mash until the potatoes are creamy.
9. Place the beef mixture in a 9x13-inch baking dish. Spread the mashed potatoes over the top and spread to cover. Bake for 30 minutes or until golden brown.

Nutrition information: Per Serving: 320 calories; 11.1g fat; 34.7g carbohydrates; 15.8g protein; 485mg sodium; 6.9g sugar

3. Guinness Chocolate Cake

This amazing Guinness Chocolate Cake combines the delicious flavors of stout beer with dark chocolate to give you an amazing dessert experience.
Serving: Serves 8
Preparation Time: 25 minutes
Ready Time: 1½ hours

Ingredients:

- 320ml can of Guinness
- 250g dark chocolate
- 200g of butter
- 400g of caster sugar
- 140g of plain flour
- 2 large eggs
- 1 teaspoon of bicarbonate of soda

Instructions:
1. Preheat the oven to 180 C / Gas 4.
2. Grease and line a 20 cm springform cake tin.
3. In a saucepan, melt together the Guinness, chocolate and butter until completely melted together.
4. In a mixing bowl, mix together the sugar, flour and eggs.
5. Pour in the melted chocolate mixture and mix until fully combined.
6. Add the bicarbonate of soda and mix until combined.
7. Pour the mixture into the prepared tin.
8. Bake in the preheated oven for 50 minutes to 1 hour, or until a skewer inserted into the center comes out clean.
9. Allow to cool before serving.

Nutrition information: 8 servings, 771 calories per serving, Fat 40g, Protein 7g, Carbohydrates 97g, Cholesterol 127mg, Sodium 197mg.

4. Guinness Braised Short Ribs

Hearty and comforting, Guinness Braised Short Ribs is an easy and delicious dish that has a rich and flavorful sauce. It's a great family dinner or a special occasion that everyone is sure to love.
Serving: 4
Preparation time: 10 minutes
Ready time: 2-3 hours

Ingredients:
• 4-5 lbs. pork short ribs
• 2 cups of Guinness beer
• 1 large onion, diced
• 2 cloves of garlic, minced

- 2 tablespoons of tomato paste
- 2 tablespoons of fresh thyme
- 2 tablespoons of Worcestershire sauce
- 1 teaspoon of smoked paprika
- 2 tablespoons of olive oil
- 1 teaspoon of salt
- 1/4 teaspoon of black pepper

Instructions:
1. Preheat oven to 350 degrees Fahrenheit.
2. Heat the olive oil in a large Dutch oven over medium heat.
3. Add the short ribs and brown on all sides, about 10 minutes.
4. Add the onion, garlic, and tomato paste and cook until the vegetables begin to soften, about 5 minutes.
5. Add the Guinness beer, thyme, Worcestershire sauce, smoked paprika, salt, and pepper to the pot and stir to combine.
6. Increase heat to high and bring the mixture to a boil.
7. Cover the pot and transfer to the preheated oven.
8. Bake for 2-3 hours, or until the short ribs are tender.
9. Carefully remove the pot from the oven and uncover.
10. Allow the short ribs to cool slightly before serving.

Nutrition information:
Serving Size: 1 Serving: Calories: 502 kcal
Carbohydrates: 5 g
Protein: 45 g
Fat: 29 g
Sodium: 843 mg
Sugar: 2 g

5. Guinness Onion Soup

Guinness Onion Soup is a delicious and savory combination of Guinness stout beer, caramelized onions, beef broth, and herbs. This hearty soup is perfect for colder months and a great dinner entree.
Serving: 4-6
Preparation time: 10 minutes
Ready time: 45 minutes

Ingredients:
- 2 tablespoons olive oil
- 2 ¼ pounds yellow onions, chopped
- 1 teaspoon fresh thyme leaves
- 2 garlic cloves, minced
- Salt and pepper to taste
- 4 cups beef broth
- 2 cups Guinness stout beer
- 4 ounces Gruyere cheese, shredded

Instructions:
1. Heat the olive oil in a large pot over medium heat.
2. Add the onions, thyme, garlic, salt, and pepper, cooking until the onions are lightly brown and caramelized, about 15 minutes.
3. Add the beef broth and Guinness stout beer, stirring to combine.
4. Bring to a boil then reduce the heat to a simmer, cooking for 25 minutes.
5. Serve the soup in bowls with a sprinkle of shredded Gruyere cheese.

Nutrition information: per serving of 147g
Calories: 172, Total Fat: 9g, Saturated Fat: 4g, Sodium: 498mg, Potassium: 444mg, Carbohydrates: 11g, Fiber: 2g, Sugar: 4g, Protein: 8g.

6. Guinness BBQ Chicken Wings

This delicious recipe for Guinness BBQ Chicken Wings is an easy to make pub-style appetizer for parties or family gatherings. These wings are coated with a tangy barbecue sauce infused with a hearty stout beer.
Serving: Makes 8-10 servings.
Preparation time: 20 minutes.
Ready time: 45 minutes.

Ingredients:
- 2 lbs. chicken wings
- 1 bottle Guinness Beer
- 1/4 cup brown sugar
- 1 teaspoon garlic powder

- 1 teaspoon chili powder
- 1/2 teaspoon smoked paprika
- 1/2 cup ketchup
- 1/4 cup white vinegar
- 1 tablespoon Worcestershire sauce
- 1 teaspoon yellow mustard
- 1/4 teaspoon ground black pepper

Instructions:
1. Preheat oven to 375°F.
2. In a medium mixing bowl, combine Guinness Beer, brown sugar, garlic powder, chili powder, and paprika; mix until well-combined.
3. Place the chicken wings on a large baking sheet lined with aluminum foil.
4. Pour the Guinness mixture over the wings and gently stir until they are completely coated.
5. Bake the wings for 25 minutes, or until they are golden brown and the sauce has reduced.
6. Increase the oven temperature to 475°F and bake the wings for an additional 15-20 minutes, until the wings are crispy and the sauce has caramelized.
7. While the wings are baking, add the ketchup, white vinegar, Worcestershire sauce, mustard, and ground black pepper to a medium saucepan. Simmer over low heat until the sauce thickens.
8. When the wings have finished baking, brush the sauce over them and serve.

Nutrition information:
Per serving: 360 calories, 20g fat, 1.7g saturated fat, 11g carbohydrates, 3g sugar, 24g protein, 0g fiber.

7. Guinness Brown Bread

This Irish classic 'Guinness Brown Bread' is a delicious alternative to white bread, with the addition of the dark beer offering a hint of bitterness. Serve this brown bread as part of a hearty breakfast or dinner - either way it will be a hit!
Serving: Makes 1 loaf

Preparation time: 10 minutes
Ready time: 1.5 hours

Ingredients:
- 1½ cups of all-purpose flour
- 1 cup whole wheat flour
- 2 teaspoons baking soda
- 2 tablespoons dark brown sugar
- 1 teaspoon salt
- 1 cup buttermilk
- 2 tablespoons vegetable oil
- 1 cup Guinness beer

Instructions:
1. Preheat oven to 350°F. Grease a 9-inch round cake pan with cooking spray.
2. In a large bowl, combine the flours, baking soda, brown sugar and salt.
3. Add the buttermilk, oil and Guinness beer to the dry Ingredients and mix until all Ingredients are moistened.
4. Pour the batter into the prepared pan and level the top. Bake for 40–45 minutes or until a toothpick inserted in the center comes out clean.
5. Cool for 10 minutes in the pan before turning out onto a cooling rack to cool completely.

Nutrition information:
- Calories:
- Fat:
- Carbohydrates:
- Protein:

8. Guinness Beef Pot Pie

Get ready for a hearty and flavorful meal with this Guinness Beef Pot Pie dish! This savory pot pie is made with tender beef, mushrooms, and veggies smothered in a delicious Guinness beer and beef broth sauce and topped off with a creamy mashed potato crust topped.
Serving: 4-6
Preparation Time: 35 minutes

Ready Time: 1 hour and 5 minutes

Ingredients:
- 2 tablespoons of olive oil
- 1 large onion, diced
- 2 cloves of garlic, minced
- 1 pound of lean ground beef or beef strips
- 1/2 teaspoon of dried rosemary
- 1 teaspoon of salt
- 1/2 teaspoon of pepper
- 8 ounces of sliced mushrooms
- 1/3 cup of all-purpose flour
- 1 cup of Guinness beer
- 1 cup of beef broth
- 3 cups of frozen mixed vegetables
- 2 cups of mashed potatoes

Instructions:
1. Preheat oven to 350°F. Heat olive oil in a large skillet over medium heat.
2. Add the onions and garlic and cook for 3 minutes.
3. Add the beef, rosemary, salt, and pepper. Cook, stirring to break up the beef, until the meat is browned and cooked through.
4. Add the mushrooms and cook for 2 minutes.
5. Sprinkle the flour over the mixture and cook for 1 minute.
6. Stir in the Guinness and beef broth and cook until the mixture bubbles and thickens.
7. Add the frozen vegetables and cook for 5 minutes.
8. Pour the mixture into a 9-inch baking dish. Top with mashed potatoes and bake for 30 minutes.

Nutrition information:
Amount Per Serving:
Calories: 386, Protein: 20g, Fiber: 8g, Total Fat: 11g, Cholesterol: 44mg, Sodium: 897mg, Total Carbohydrates: 38g

9. Guinness Chocolate Brownies

Deliciously fudgy brownies made with Guinness and semi-sweet chocolate, these Guinness Chocolate Brownies are sure to please chocoholics everywhere!
Serving: 16 pieces
Preparation time: 15 minutes
Ready time: 45 minutes

Ingredients:
• 2/3 cup Guinness beer
• 4 ounces semi-sweet chocolate, cut into small pieces
• 2 tablespoons unsalted butter
• 2 large eggs, at room temperature
• 1 cup sugar
• 1 teaspoon vanilla extract
• 3/4 cup all-purpose flour
• 1/4 teaspoon salt
• 3 ounces semi-sweet chocolate chips

Instructions:
1. Preheat oven to 350°F. Grease an 8-inch square baking pan.
2. In a small saucepan, heat Guinness and butter over medium heat until butter is melted and mixture is bubbling.
3. Remove saucepan from heat and add chocolate pieces, stirring until melted.
4. In a large bowl, whisk together eggs, sugar, and vanilla until combined.
5. Add chocolate mixture and whisk until combined.
6. Add flour and salt and gently fold together.
7. Stir in chocolate chips.
8. Pour batter into greased baking pan and spread evenly.
9. Bake for 36-40 minutes, until a toothpick inserted in the center comes out clean.
10. Cool in pan for 15 minutes before cutting into pieces.

Nutrition information: 40 calories, 1.5g fat, 6g carbohydrates, 0.5g protein per brownie.

10. Guinness Marinated Steak

This dish is a delicious combination of the classic steak-and-Guinness flavors, perfect for any special occasion or meal.
Serving: 4
Preparation Time: 10 minutes
Ready Time: 45 minutes

Ingredients:
• 2 lbs sirloin steak, cut into 1.5-inch cubes
• 3 cloves garlic, minced
• 1 teaspoon ground black pepper
• 2 tablespoons olive oil
• 2 cups Guinness stout beer
• 1 cup beef stock
• 2 tablespoons Worcestershire sauce
• 2 tablespoons butter
• 2 tablespoons fresh parsley, chopped

Instructions:
1. In a large bowl, combine the steak cubes, garlic, black pepper, and olive oil. Mix well and set aside.
2. In a separate bowl, combine the Guinness, beef stock, and Worcestershire sauce.
3. Preheat a large skillet over medium-high heat. Add the steak cubes and cook until browned, about 5 minutes. Add the beer mixture to the skillet and bring to a simmer. Simmer for 25–30 minutes until the steak is cooked through and the sauce has reduced by half.
4. Reduce the heat to low, add the butter and parsley, and stir until the butter has melted.
5. Serve the Guinness-marinated steak over mashed potatoes or rice, and enjoy.

Nutrition information (per serving):
• Calories: 550
• Protein: 36 grams
• Fat: 30 grams
• Carbs: 13 grams

11. Guinness Lamb Stew

Guinness Lamb Stew is a delicious and hearty dish featuring fall-apart tender lamb with vegetables and a delicious sauce. It's a perfect comforting meal for the cooler months.
Serving: 4-6
Preparation Time: 30 minutes
Ready Time: 3 hours

Ingredients:
- 2 lbs. lamb shoulder cubes
- 2 onions, chopped
- 3 cloves of garlic, minced
- 2 large carrots, chopped
- 2 stalks of celery, chopped
- 2 tablespoons of tomato paste
- 1 bottle of Guinness stout
- 2 tablespoons of Worcestershire sauce
- 2 sprigs of fresh thyme
- 2 tablespoons of olive oil
- Salt and pepper to taste

Instructions:
1. Heat a large Dutch oven over medium-high heat. Add the olive oil and the pieces of lamb. Season the lamb with salt and pepper. Brown the lamb on all sides, about 5 minutes.
2. Remove the lamb and set aside. Add the chopped onions, carrots, celery, and garlic to the pot. Sauté for 5-7 minutes, until vegetables are softened.
3. Add the tomato paste, Guinness stout, Worcestershire sauce, and thyme to the vegetables. Stir until everything is combined.
4. Return the lamb to the pot and bring to a simmer. Cover the pot and reduce heat to low. Simmer stew for 2 to 3 hours, until the meat is tender and sauce has reduced.
5. Serve the stew with crusty bread and enjoy!

Nutrition information: (Per Serving)
Calories: 311 kcal, Protein: 28 g, Fat: 17 g, Sodium: 127 mg, Carbohydrates: 14 g, Fiber: 4 g

12. Guinness Chocolate Mousse

Indulge in a rich and decadent treat with this creamy Guinness Chocolate Mousse. The creamy chocolate blend is lightened with a hint of Guinness beer, making for a delicious dessert to enjoy.
Serving: 4
Preparation Time: 5 minutes
Ready Time: 15 minutes

Ingredients:
3/4 cup semisweet chocolate chips
2/3 cup heavy cream
1/2 teaspoon instant espresso powder
2 tablespoons Guinness stout beer

Instructions:
1. In a medium bowl, melt the chocolate chips in the microwave in 30 second intervals, stirring in between to ensure the chocolate melts evenly.
2. In a separate bowl, whip heavy cream until medium peaks form.
3. Add the espresso powder to the melted chocolate and stir to combine.
4. Gently fold in the Guinness beer, followed by the whipped cream.
5. Divide the mousse among four serving dishes, cover with plastic wrap, and refrigerate for at least 15 minutes before serving.

Nutrition information: calories: 256, fat: 22g

13. Guinness Battered Fish and Chips

Enjoy a fulfilling meal with this delicious Guinness-Battered Fish & Chips recipe. It's an irresistible combination of crispy fried fish coated with a Guinness beer batter and served with crunchy chips and malt vinegar.
Serving: 4
Preparation time: 15 minutes
Ready Time: 30 minutes

Ingredients:

- 1 can of Guinness Draught
- 2 cups plain flour
- 2 teaspoons baking powder
- 1 teaspoon black pepper
- 2 large potatoes
- 2 tablespoons malt vinegar
- 2-3 fillets of white fish
- 1 teaspoon of salt
- Vegetable oil, for deep-frying

Instructions:
1. Preheat vegetable oil in a deep-fryer or a large, deep pot.
2. Peel and size the potatoes, and place them in a pot of salted water. Simmer until the potatoes are tender, about 8 minutes.
3. In a large bowl, combine the Guinness, flour, baking powder, and pepper. Stir together until the batter is smooth.
4. Dip each fillet of fish into the batter and gently place in the preheated oil. Fry until golden brown and cooked through, about 5 minutes.
5. Remove the chips from the pot and drain them on a paper towel. Fry them in the hot oil until golden brown and crispy.
6. Serve the fish and chips with malt vinegar on the side.

Nutrition information: 870 calories, 36g fat, 48g carbohydrates, 30g protein.

14. Guinness Irish Soda Bread

Guinness Irish Soda Bread is a moist, dense bread that is traditional in Irish cuisine. It is made with minimal Ingredients and is perfect for breakfast or an afternoon snack.
Serving: 14
Preparation time: 15 minutes
Ready time: 75 minutes

Ingredients:
- 4 cups all-purpose flour
- 4 tablespoons white sugar
- 2 teaspoons baking soda

- 1 teaspoon kosher salt
- 12 ounces Guinness Draught
- 3 tablespoons unsalted butter, melted
- 2 large eggs, beaten
- ¾ cup raisins (optional)

Instructions:
1. Preheat the oven to 350 degrees F. Grease and flour an 8-inch round cake pan.
2. In a large bowl, whisk together the flour, sugar, baking soda, and salt.
3. Stir in the Guinness, melted butter, and beaten eggs until a dough forms. Fold in the raisins if using.
4. Transfer the dough into the prepared pan and bake for 60-75 minutes, or until a toothpick inserted in the middle comes out clean.
5. Allow the bread to cool in the pan for 10 minutes, then turn out and cool completely on a wire rack.

Nutrition information: Servings – 14, Calories - 216, Fat – 8g, Cholesterol - 51mg, Sodium – 529mg, Carbohydrates – 31g, Protein – 6g.

15. Guinness Braised Brisket

Guinness Braised Brisket is a rich and delicious Irish-inspired dish made with beef brisket that is slow cooked in a delicious Guinness gravy.
Serving: 6-8
Preparation time: 15 minutes
Ready time: 5 hours

Ingredients:
• 3-4 lbs beef brisket
• 5 cloves garlic, minced
• 1 onion, diced
• 2 cups beef stock
• 1 bottle Guinness
• Salt and pepper to taste

Instructions:

1. Preheat oven to 325°F.
2. Season the brisket with salt and pepper and place it in a large ovenproof pot.
3. Add the garlic, onion, beef stock, and Guinness to the pot and stir well.
4. Cover the pot and place in the preheated oven.
5. Braise for 4-5 hours, or until the brisket is tender and easily shreds with a fork.
6. Remove from the oven and shred the brisket, discarding any fat.
7. Return the shreds to the sauce and stir to coat.
8. Serve hot.

Nutrition information:
Serving size: 1/8th of brisket
Calories: 368 Protein: 37.4g Fat: 16.6g Carbohydrates: 8.6g Fiber: 0.3g
Sodium: 524mg

16. Guinness Chocolate Truffles

Guinness Chocolate Truffles are a unique spin on the traditional chocolate truffle. These boozy, rich and creamy treats are perfect for St. Patrick's Day or any special occasion.
Serving: Makes 4 dozen truffles
Preparation Time: 30 minutes
Ready Time: 4 hours

Ingredients:
- 8 ounces semi sweet chocolate chips
- 2/3 cup heavy cream
- 1 shot of whiskey
- 1/2 cup Guinness Stout beer
- 1 teaspoon vanilla extract
- For dusting, cocoa powder

Instructions:
1. Place chocolate chips in a heatproof bowl.

2. In a small saucepan, heat the cream, whiskey, Guinness and vanilla extract over medium-high heat. Once the mixture reaches a simmer, reduce the heat to low and stir for 3 minutes.

3. Pour the cream mixture over the chocolate chips and let sit for 2 minutes.

4. Stir until all the Ingredients are incorporated. Once all the chocolate chips are melted and the mixture is smooth, pour it into an 8x8 inch baking dish.

5. Refrigerate for at least 4 hours until the mixture is hardened.

6. Use a melon-baller or spoon to scoop out 1-inch portions of the chocolate mixture.

7. Roll each truffle into a ball with your hands and coat with cocoa powder. Refrigerate until ready to serve.

Nutrition information:
Per Serving: 119 calories, 8.2g fat, 10.7g sugar, 0.9g protein, 0.3g fiber, 5.3mg cholesterol.

17. Guinness BBQ Ribs

Guinness BBQ Ribs are a delicious combination of marinated ribs that are slow cooked and finished with a Guinness BBQ sauce with a hint of smokiness and sweetness.

Serving: 4
Preparation time: 10 minutes
Ready time: 2 hours

Ingredients:
• 2 Racks of Pork Ribs
• 4 Cloves of Garlic, Minced
• 1/4 Cup of Soy Sauce
• 1/4 Cup of Brown Sugar
• 2 Cans of Guinness
• 1 Cup of Ketchup
• 1/4 Cup of Apple Cider Vinegar
• 1/4 Cup of Worcestershire Sauce

Instructions:

1. Preheat the oven to 350°F.
2. Mix the garlic, soy sauce, brown sugar, and one can of Guinness in a large bowl to make the marinade.
3. Place the ribs in a baking dish and cover them with the marinade. Cover the dish with aluminum foil and bake for one hour.
4. In a saucepan, combine the remaining Guinness, ketchup, vinegar, and Worcestershire sauce. Simmer for 20 minutes.
5. Remove the ribs from the oven and brush them with the Guinness BBQ sauce.
6. Preheat the grill to high and place the ribs on the grill, flip every 3 minutes for 12 minutes or until cooked through.
7. Slice the ribs and serve with the remaining Guinness BBQ sauce.

Nutrition information: Calories- 585, Fat- 31.5g, Cholesterol- 100mg, Sodium- 1973mg, Carbohydrates- 29.5g, Protein- 37.9g.

18. Guinness Irish Stew

Guinness Irish stew is a traditional stew made with beef, potatoes, onions and vegetables simmered in a rich, flavorful Guinness beer broth. This hearty and comforting classic is easy to make and can be enjoyed all year round.
Serving: Serves 6
Preparation time: 10 minutes
Ready time: 1 hour 30 minutes

Ingredients:
- 2 tablespoons vegetable oil
- 2 1/2 pounds beef chuck roast, cut into 1 inch cubes
- Salt and freshly ground black pepper
- 2 large onions finely chopped
- 4 large carrots, peeled and diced
- 4 cloves garlic, minced
- 1 tablespoon tomato paste
- 2 cups beef broth
- 2 (14.9-ounce) cans Guinness Extra Stout Beer
- 2 bay leaves
- 2 tablespoons Worcestershire sauce

- 5 red potatoes, cut into 1 inch cubes

Instructions:
1. Heat the oil in a large soup pot over medium-high heat. Season the beef cubes liberally with salt and pepper.
2. Add the beef to the hot pan and sear on all sides until the beef cubes are browned.
3. Add the onions, carrots, and garlic and cook until the vegetables are soft and aromatic, about 5 minutes. Stir in the tomato paste until it coats the vegetables.
4. Pour in the beef broth, Guinness Extra Stout, bay leaves, and Worcestershire sauce and stir to combine.
5. Bring the stew to a boil, then reduce the heat to low and simmer for 1 hour.
6. Add the potatoes to the stew and simmer for another 30 minutes, or until the potatoes are cooked through.
7. Taste the stew and adjust seasoning with salt and pepper, if necessary. Discard the bay leaves before serving.

Nutrition information:
Calories: 464 kcal; Fat: 17.2 g; Carbohydrates: 32.5 g; Protein: 34.6 g; Cholesterol: 89 mg; Sodium: 563 mg

19. Guinness Chocolate Pudding

This delicious Guinness Chocolate Pudding is a great treat to whip up for special occasions. It is rich in flavour, with a creamy texture, and is sure to be enjoyed by all.
Serving: This recipe serves 4.
Preparation Time: 25 mins
Ready Time: 45 mins

Ingredients:
- ½ cup Guinness beer
- 4 tablespoons cocoa powder
- 2 tablespoons cornstarch
- ¾ cup granulated sugar
- 2 cups whole milk

- 4 tablespoons butter
- ½ teaspoon vanilla extract
- Pinch of salt

Instructions:
1. In a medium saucepan, whisk together the Guinness, cocoa powder, cornstarch, and sugar until smooth.
2. Slowly add the milk, stirring continuously to prevent lumps from forming.
3. Place the saucepan over low-medium heat and bring to a gentle simmer, stirring continuously.
4. When the mixture begins to thicken, add the butter, vanilla extract, and salt. Simmer, stirring often, for 4-5 minutes, until thickened and smooth.
5. Remove the pudding from the heat and transfer it to a serving bowl. Allow to cool for 10-15 minutes before serving.

Nutrition information: Per serving this recipe contains 226 calories, 9.3g fat, 28.5g sugar, and 4.3g protein.

20. Guinness Braised Pork Belly

Guinness Braised Pork Belly is an Irish-inspired dish that uses fatty pork belly and a dark beer to create a flavorful and unique meal.
Serving: 4 people
Preparation Time: 25 minutes
Ready Time: 4 hours

Ingredients:
- 2 pounds pork belly, cut into cubes
- 2 tablespoons olive oil
- 2 onions, chopped
- 4 cloves garlic, minced
- 2 tablespoons tomato paste
- 2 tablespoons fresh thyme leaves
- 1/2 teaspoon black pepper
- 2 cups Guinness
- 2 cups chicken broth

- 1/2 cup dark brown sugar

Instructions:
1. Heat the oil in a large pot and add the pork cubes. Cook over medium-high heat until the pork is just lightly browned.
2. Add the onions, garlic, tomato paste, thyme, and pepper and stir into the pork. Cook for 5 minutes, stirring occasionally.
3. Pour in the Guinness and chicken broth. Stir in the brown sugar.
4. Reduce heat to low and let simmer for 3-4 hours, stirring occasionally.
5. Serve with mashed potatoes or crusty bread.

Nutrition information: Per Serving: 442 calories, 18g fat, 24g carbohydrates, 35g protein.

21. Guinness Bangers and Mash

Guinness Bangers and Mash is a classic Irish dish made with pork sausages, potatoes and other vegetables. It is cooked in creamy Guinness beer and served with a beef sauce, which makes it a hearty and delicious meal.
Serving: 6
Preparation time: 10 minutes
Ready time: 1 hour

Ingredients:
• 6 pork sausages
• 4 potatoes, peeled and diced
• 1 onion, diced
• 2 carrots, peeled and diced
• 3 cups of beef stock
• 2 cups of Guinness beer
• 2 tablespoons of butter
• Salt and pepper to taste

Instructions:
1. Preheat the oven to 400 degrees F.
2. Place the sausages, potatoes, onions, and carrots in a roasting pan.

3. In a small bowl, mix the beef stock and Guinness beer together, and pour over the sausage and vegetables in the roasting pan.
4. Dot with butter and season with salt and pepper.
5. Bake in preheated oven for 45 minutes, or until the sausages and potatoes are cooked through and golden brown.
6. Serve with a beef sauce for a delicious and hearty meal.

Nutrition information: Per serving this dish contains approximately 319 calories, 17 g fat, 6 g carbohydrates, 28 g protein.

22. Guinness Chocolate Cheesecake

Guinness Chocolate Cheesecake is a rich and creamy chocolaty dessert with a hint of Guinness flavour. It's a truly decadent treat that will please everyone.
Serving: 8
Preparation Time: 45 minutes
Ready Time: 2 hours

Ingredients:
Crust:
• 1 1/2 cups Oreo cookie crumbs
• 2 tablespoons butter, melted
Filling:
• 16 ounces cream cheese, softened
• 1/2 cup white sugar
• 1 teaspoon vanilla extract
• Dash of salt
• 2 eggs
• 1/2 cup Guinness
• 2 cups semi-sweet or dark chocolate chips
• 1/4 cup heavy cream

Instructions:
1. Preheat oven to 375 degrees F (190 degrees C).
2. In a medium bowl, mix together the cookie crumbs and butter until evenly combined. Press into the bottom of a 9-inch springform pan.

3. In another bowl, beat cream cheese until light and fluffy. Gradually add sugar, beating until smooth. Beat in egss one at a time, followed by the Guinness and s;t.

4. Melt the chocolate chips with the cream in a double boiler or microwave safe bowl. Add to the cream cheese mixture and beat until smooth. Pour the filling into the crust.

5. Bake for 30 to 35 minutes or until the center is slightly jiggly. Allow to cool on the counter for 1 hour, then refrigerate for an additional hour.

Nutrition information:
Calories: 496, Total Fat: 33g, Saturated Fat: 20g, Cholesterol: 97mg, Sodium: 221mg, Carbohydrates: 42g, Protein: 7g

23. Guinness Glazed Salmon

This delicious dish will make any dinner party complete. It features the bold and malty flavor of Guinness beer, coupled with a zesty glaze.
Serving: 4
Preparation time
15 minutes
Ready time
25 minutes

Ingredients:
• 4 salmon fillets
• 3 tablespoons olive oil
• 1 teaspoon garlic, minced
• 2 teaspoons Dijon mustard
• 1 tablespoon honey
• 2 tablespoons Guinness beer
• Salt & pepper

Instructions:
1. Preheat your oven to 400 degrees F.
2. In a small bowl, mix olive oil, garlic, mustard, honey, Guinness and a pinch of salt & pepper.
3. Place salmon fillets in a baking tray and cover generously with the glaze.

4. Bake in the oven for 15-20 minutes, depending on the thickness of the fillets.

Nutrition information
Calories: 340 | Fat: 18 g | Carbs: 4 g | Protein: 33 g

24. Guinness Beef Chili

Guinness Beef Chili is a full-flavored chili that's made with Guinness beer and is sure to be a hit with chili fans.
Serving: 6-8
Preparation Time: 15 minutes
Ready Time: 1 hour

Ingredients:
- 2 tablespoons vegetable oil
- 2 lbs. ground beef
- 2 onions, diced
- 4 large garlic cloves, minced
- 1 jalapeno, seeded and diced
- 1 (14.9 ounce) can Guinness beer
- 2 cans (14.5 ounces each) diced tomatoes
- 2 tablespoons Worcestershire sauce
- 2 tablespoons tomato paste
- 2 tablespoons chili powder
- 1 teaspoon cumin
- 1 teaspoon smoked paprika
- 2 teaspoons salt
- 1 teaspoon black pepper
- 1/2 teaspoon cayenne pepper
- 1 (15 ounce) can kidney beans, rinsed and drained

Instructions:
1. Heat the oil in a large pot or Dutch oven over medium-high heat.
2. Add the beef and cook until browned, about 6 minutes. Once cooked, transfer the beef to a bowl and set aside.
3. Add the onions, garlic, and jalapeno to the pot and cook until softened, about 5 minutes.

4. Return the beef to the pot and stir in the Guinness beer, tomatoes, Worcestershire sauce, tomato paste, chili powder, cumin, smoked paprika, salt, pepper, and cayenne pepper.
5. Bring the mixture to a boil, reduce the heat to low, and simmer, covered, for 30 minutes.
6. Stir in the kidney beans, cover, and cook for 10 more minutes.
7. Serve with desired toppings.

Nutrition information: Per serving: 479 calories, 28g fat, 19g carbohydrates, 38g protein.

25. Guinness Chocolate Chip Cookies

Enjoy chewy, slightly bittersweet Guinness Chocolate Chip Cookies that are loaded with oatmeal, dark chocolate chips, dried fruit, and, of course, your favorite dark beer.
Serving: Makes about 2 dozen medium-sized cookies
Preparation Time: 15 minutes
Ready Time: 25 minutes

Ingredients:
• ½ cup firmly packed light brown sugar
• ½ cup granulated sugar
• ½ cup (1 stick) unsalted butter, at room temperature
• 2 large eggs
• ½ cup Guinness draught beer
• 1 teaspoon vanilla extract
• 2 ½ cups all-purpose flour
• 1 teaspoon baking soda
• ½ teaspoon salt
• 2 cups old-fashioned rolled oats
• 1 cup chopped dried fruit (apricots, figs, dates, etc.)
• 1 cup semi-sweet or dark chocolate chips

Instructions:
1. Preheat oven to 375°F. Line baking sheets with parchment paper.
2. Cream sugars and butter together until light and fluffy, about 3 minutes.

3. Beat in eggs one at a time, then stir in Guinness and vanilla.

4. In a separate bowl, whisk together flour, baking soda, and salt.

5. With mixer on low, slowly add dry Ingredients to creamed mixture, beating until combined.

6. Fold oats, dried fruit, and chocolate chips into dough using a rubber spatula.

7. Drop by heaping tablespoonful onto prepared baking sheets.

8. Bake cookies for 8–10 minutes, or until edges are golden brown.

9. Transfer cookies to a cooling rack. Enjoy!

Nutrition information: (per cookie) Calories: 153, Fat: 6.7g, Sodium: 99mg, Carbs: 22.2g, Protein: 1.4g

26. Guinness Braised Chicken

Guinness Braised Chicken is an Irish classic that combines the robust flavors of Guinness and mirepoix vegetables with savory, tender chicken for a hearty dinner that's sure to please.

Serving: Serves 4

Preparation Time: 10 minutes

Ready Time: 45 minutes

Ingredients:
- 4 boneless, skinless chicken thighs
- 2 tablespoons olive oil
- 1 small onion, chopped
- 2 carrots, chopped
- 2 celery stalks, chopped
- 2 cloves garlic, minced
- 2 cups low-sodium chicken broth
- 12 ounces Guinness beer
- 2 sprigs fresh thyme
- 2 sprigs fresh rosemary
- 2 teaspoons cornstarch
- kosher salt and freshly ground black pepper, to taste

Instructions:

1. Heat olive oil in a large skillet over medium high heat. Place chicken thighs in the skillet and cook for 6-8 minutes, flipping once, until evenly browned.
2. Add the onion, carrots, celery and garlic to the skillet. Cook, stirring occasionally, until the vegetables are softened, about 3-5 minutes.
3. Pour chicken broth and Guinness into the skillet. Add the thyme and rosemary. Bring to a boil then reduce heat to low, cover and simmer for 20-25 minutes, or until the chicken is cooked through.
4. In a small bowl, whisk the cornstarch with 2 tablespoons of cold water then pour into the skillet. Stir it into the sauce and simmer until the sauce has slightly thickened.
5. Serve chicken with roasted potatoes or overcooked pasta.

Nutrition information:
Calories: 261kcal, Carbohydrates: 7g, Protein: 23g, Fat: 14g, Saturated Fat: 3g, Cholesterol: 89mg, Sodium: 343mg, Potassium: 489mg, Fiber: 1g, Sugar: 2g, Vitamin A: 3111IU, Vitamin C: 7mg, Calcium: 42mg, Iron: 2mg

27. Guinness Chocolate Ice Cream

Guinness Chocolate Ice Cream is a fantastic dessert that combines the bold taste of Guinness beer with the sweetness of chocolate for a delicious treat.
Serving: Approximately 6 servings
Preparation Time: 15 minutes
Ready Time: 6 - 8 hours

Ingredients:
- 3 cups of heavy cream
- 1 cup of Guinness beer
- ⅔ cup of cocoa powder
- ½ cup of sugar
- 1 teaspoon of vanilla extract

Instructions:
1. In a bowl, whisk together the cocoa powder and Guinness beer until well blended.

2. In a separate bowl, beat the heavy cream until soft peaks form.

3. Add the sugar and vanilla extract to the whipped cream and mix until combined.

4. Gently fold in the Guinness and cocoa powder mixture until everything is incorporated.

5. Taste and adjust sweetness as needed.

6. Place the ice cream mixture in a freezer-safe container and freeze for 6-8 hours.

7. Once frozen, let the ice cream sit for 15 minutes before scooping.

Nutrition information: Per serving (1/2 cup): Calories: 234, Total Fat: 17g (Saturated Fat: 11g), Cholesterol: 62mg, Sodium: 14mg, Carbohydrates: 16g (Fiber: 2g, Sugar: 12g), Protein: 4g

28. Guinness Beef Sliders

These tasty Guinness Beef Sliders are the perfect treat for the beer-lover in your life. Packed with flavor and easy to make, these iconic sliders will have your guests smiling from the first bite.

Serving: 8 Sliders

Preparation Time: 15 minutes

Ready Time: 25 minutes

Ingredients:
- 2 tablespoons vegetable oil
- 1-pound ground beef
- 1 small onion, diced
- 1 clove garlic, minced
- 1 teaspoon ground cumin
- ½ teaspoon smoked paprika
- ¼ teaspoon cayenne pepper
- 1/3 cup Guinness beer
- 2 tablespoons ketchup
- 2 tablespoons Worcestershire sauce
- 1 teaspoon Dijon mustard
- ¼ teaspoon salt
- 1/8 teaspoon black pepper
- 8 slider buns

- Shredded lettuce
- Sliced tomatoes
- Sliced pickles
- Ketchup, mustard and mayonnaise (optional)

Instructions:
1. Heat oil in a large skillet over medium-high heat. Add the ground beef, onion, garlic, cumin, smoked paprika and cayenne pepper. Cook for 10 minutes, stirring occasionally, until the beef is cooked through and the onion is fragrant.
2. Add the Guinness, ketchup, Worcestershire sauce, Dijon mustard, salt and pepper. Bring to a simmer and cook for another 3 minutes.
3. To assemble the sliders, spoon the beef mixture onto the slider rolls and top with lettuce, tomatoes, pickles, ketchup, mustard and mayonnaise. Serve immediately.

Nutrition information: Nutritional information per one slider is approximately 190 calories, 8 grams of fat, 17 grams of carbohydrates and 10 grams of protein.

29. Guinness Chocolate Fudge

Guiness Chocolate Fudge is a rich, decadent dessert combining two delicious flavors. It is easy to make and can be served with a scoop of ice cream or a dollop of whipped cream.
Serving: 8
Preparation time: 10 minutes
Ready time: 2 hours

Ingredients:
- 1 (14 ounce) can sweetened condensed milk
- 2 tablespoons butter
- 1/2 cup Guinness Stout
- 2 cups semi-sweet or bittersweet chocolate chips

Instructions:
1. In a medium-sized saucepan, combine condensed milk, butter and Guinness.

2. Heat over medium-low heat until butter melts and mixture starts to bubble.
3. Add the chocolate chips and continue to stir gently until melted.
4. Pour the mixture into a greased 8-inch square baking pan and let cool for about 2 hours.
5. Cut into squares and serve.

Nutrition information (per 1/8 of fudge): 320 cals, 21 g fat, 79 mg sodium, 35 g carbs, 3 g protein

30. Guinness Braised Lamb Shanks

'Guinness Braised Lamb Shanks" is a delicious and savory dish that is sure to warm the soul. Slow cooked in a mixture of Guinness beer and spices, this dish is a real crowd pleaser.
Serving: 4
Preparation time: 20 minutes
Ready time: 2 hours

Ingredients:
• 4 lamb shanks
• 2 tablespoons olive oil
• 2 large onions, diced
• 2 cloves garlic, minced
• 2 tablespoons tomato paste
• 2 tablespoons fresh rosemary, chopped
• 2 tablespoons fresh thyme, chopped
• 2 cups Guinness beer
• 2 cups beef stock
• 2 bay leaves
• 1 tablespoon brown sugar
• Salt and pepper, to taste

Instructions:
1. Preheat oven to 375°F.
2. Heat the olive oil in a large Dutch oven over medium-high heat. Add the onions, and sauté until softened and lightly browned, about 5 minutes. Add the garlic and tomato paste, and sauté for another minute.

3. Add the lamb shanks, rosemary, thyme, Guinness, beef stock, bay leaves, brown sugar, salt and pepper, and bring to a gentle boil.
4. Cover the pot and place it in the preheated oven.
5. Braise in the oven for 1 1/2 to 2 hours, or until the lamb shanks are fall-apart tender.
6. Serve with your favorite sides.

Nutrition information:
Calories:369.1, Fat: 8.6 g, Saturated fat: 2.6 g, Carbohydrates: 10.9 g, Sugar: 4.2 g, Fiber: 0.4 g, Protein: 32.0 g, Cholesterol: 71.7 mg, Sodium: 119.2 mg

31. Guinness Chocolate Cupcakes

These Guinness Chocolate Cupcakes are the perfect indulgence. Rich chocolate cupcakes with a hint of Guinness stout and covered in a creamy, chocolate-Guinness frosting. Serving: 12 cupcakes. Preparation time: 15 minutes. Ready time: 45 minutes.

Ingredients:
- 2 1/2 cups all-purpose flour
- 2/3 cup cocoa powder
- 2 teaspoons baking soda
- 1/4 teaspoon salt
- 1 cup (2 sticks) unsalted butter, at room temperature
- 2 cups granulated sugar
- 2 large eggs, at room temperature
- 1 teaspoon vanilla extract
- 1 cup Guinness stout beer
- 8 ounces semi-sweet chocolate chips
- 4 ounces unsweetened chocolate, chopped

Instructions:
1. Preheat oven to 350° F. Line a 12-cup muffin tin with paper liners and set aside.
2. In a large bowl, sift together the flour, cocoa powder, baking soda, and salt. Set aside.

3. In a large mixing bowl, cream together the butter and sugar until light and fluffy.

4. Add the eggs one at a time, scraping down the sides of the bowl between each addition.

5. Add the vanilla extract and the Guinness stout and mix until fully incorporated.

6. Add the dry Ingredients and mix until combined.

7. Gently fold in the chocolate chips and chopped chocolate.

8. Scoop the batter into prepared muffin tin, filling each cup about 3/4 of the way.

9. Bake for 18-20 minutes, or until a toothpick inserted into the center of a cupcake comes out clean.

10. Allow cupcakes to cool completely before frosting.

Nutrition information: Per serving (1 cupcake): Calories: 355; Fat: 16g; Saturated Fat: 10g; Cholesterol: 54mg; Sodium: 165mg; Carbohydrates: 49g; Fiber: 2g; Protein: 4g.

32. Guinness Guinness-Battered Onion Rings

Guinness and onion rings have long been savored together, but the Guinness Guinness-Battered Onion Rings take it up a notch with a deep fried beer-battered version. Enjoy the savory crunch and the delicious flavor of Guinness in a unique form.

Serving: 4-6

Preparation time: 10 minutes

Ready time: 25 minutes

Ingredients:
- 1 large onion, sliced into 1/2-inch thick rings
- 4 ounces Guinness stout
- 1 ¼ cups all-purpose flour
- 1 teaspoon ground cumin
- 2 teaspoons garlic powder
- 1 teaspoon baking powder
- 1 teaspoon fine sea salt
- 1 teaspoon ground black pepper
- 1 cup panko bread crumbs

- 1 egg
- Vegetable oil, for deep frying

Instructions:
1. Place the onion rings in a shallow dish.
2. In a separate bowl, whisk together the Guinness, flour, cumin, garlic powder, baking powder, salt, and pepper.
3. Once the batter is smooth, stir in the panko and egg.
4. Dip the onion rings in the Guinness batter, making sure to coat evenly.
5. Heat the vegetable oil in a deep skillet or deep fryer to 375°F.
6. Carefully place the battered onion rings in the hot oil and fry for 4 to 6 minutes, turning occasionally to ensure even cooking.
7. Remove the onion rings from the oil and let them drain on a plate lined with paper towels.
8. Serve immediately while still hot with your favorite condiment.

Nutrition information:
Calories: 149 kcal; Protein: 4 g; Fat: 5 g; Sat. Fat: 1 g; Carbs: 18 g; Fiber: 1 g; Sugars: 1 g; Sodium: 419 mg

33. Guinness Chocolate Milkshake

This Guinness Chocolate Milkshake is a delightful combination of rich chocolate and deep, roasted Guinness flavors. The combination of these two unique flavors creates a smooth and decadent milkshake that just can't be beat!
Serving: Makes 5 servings
Preparation Time: 10 minutes
Ready Time: 20 minutes

Ingredients:
- 2 cups ice
- 1 cup Guinness Stout
- 2 tablespoons cocoa powder
- 2 tablespoons brown sugar
- ½ cup heavy cream
- 1 cup semi-sweet chocolate chips

- 2 cups vanilla ice cream

Instructions:
1. In a blender, combine ice, Guinness, cocoa powder, brown sugar, cream, and chocolate chips. Blend until all Ingredients are well combined.
2. Add in the vanilla ice cream and blend until a thick milkshake consistency is reached.
3. Divide the milkshake into 5 glasses and serve.

Nutrition information:
Calories: 384, Total Fat: 24 g, Saturated Fat: 14 g, Cholesterol: 61 mg, Sodium: 78 mg, Carbohydrates: 33 g, Fiber: 2 g, Sugar: 18 g, Protein: 7 g

34. Guinness Pulled Pork

Guinness Pulled Pork is a classic slow-cooked dish made with dark stout beer and pork shoulder. The pork is cooked until it is fork tender and then shredded and served with hamburger buns for an amazing sandwich.
Serving: 6-8
Preparation time: 15 minutes
Ready time: 6 hours

Ingredients:
• 3 lb boneless pork shoulder
• 2 cloves garlic, minced
• 2 tablespoons dark brown sugar
• 2 teaspoons each of paprika, garlic powder, and onion powder
• 1 teaspoon each of dried thyme and ground black pepper
• 1 teaspoons ground cumin
• 1 bottle Guinness stout beer
• ¼ cup apple cider vinegar
• ¼ cup molasses
• ½ cup ketchup

Instructions:
1. Preheat the oven to 275 degrees F.

2. In a large bowl, combine the minced garlic, brown sugar, paprika, garlic powder, onion powder, thyme, pepper, and cumin.
3. Rub the spice mixture all over the pork shoulders.
4. Place the pork shoulders in a large baking dish.
5. Pour in the Guinness stout, apple cider vinegar, molasses, and ketchup.
6. Cook in the preheated oven for 6 hours until the pork is tender and easily shreddable with a fork.
7. Remove from the oven and allow to cool for 10 minutes before beginning to shred the pork.
8. Serve the Guinness Pulled Pork on hamburger buns with coleslaw, pickles, and other desired toppings.

Nutrition information:
Calories: 276 kcal, Carbohydrates: 14 g, Protein: 31 g, Fat: 8 g, Saturated Fat: 2 g, Cholesterol: 95 mg, Sodium: 275 mg, Potassium: 523 mg, Sugar: 12 g, Vitamin A: 233 IU, Vitamin C: 1 mg, Calcium: 38 mg, Iron: 2 mg

35. Guinness Chocolate Pancakes

Guinness Chocolate Pancakes are a unique breakfast treat! They are made with beer, cocoa and other goodies, making them light and fluffy and giving them an amazing flavor. Serve these savory and sweet pancakes to friends and family for a special brunch dish.
Serving: 4-6
Preparation Time: 15 minutes
Ready Time: 20 minutes

Ingredients:
- 2 cups Guinness stout beer
- 1 1/2 cups all-purpose flour
- 1/4 cup cocoa powder
- 2 tablespoons white sugar
- 1 teaspoon baking soda
- 1/4 teaspoon salt
- 2 large eggs
- 2 tablespoons melted butter
- 1 cup buttermilk

Instructions:
1. In a large bowl, combine the Guinness, flour, cocoa powder, sugar, baking soda and salt.
2. In a separate bowl, whisk together the eggs, melted butter and buttermilk.
3. Slowly add the wet Ingredients to the dry Ingredients, stirring until just combined.
4. Heat a lightly greased griddle or large non-stick skillet over medium heat.
5. Drop the batter onto the pan in 1/4 cup portions, flipping when bubbles form on the surface and the pancakes are golden brown on the bottom.
6. Serve with butter and syrup, if desired.

Nutrition information (per serving):
Calories: 239 kcal, Carbohydrates: 33 g, Protein: 8 g, Fat: 6 g, Saturated Fat: 2 g, Cholesterol: 67 mg, Sodium: 478 mg, Potassium: 158 mg, Fiber: 2 g, Sugar: 6 g, Vitamin A: 221 IU, Calcium: 62 mg, Iron: 2 mg

36. Guinness Braised Duck Legs

Guinness Braised Duck Legs are a flavorful and comforting dish that is perfect for any special occasion or a cozy night in. The deliciously rich flavor comes from slowly simmering the duck legs in a full-bodied stout beer like Guinness, making for an unforgettable dish.
Serving: 4
Preparation time: 10 minutes
Ready time: 2 hours and 10 minutes

Ingredients:
- 2 tablespoons olive oil
- 4 duck legs
- 2 onions, diced
- 2 carrots, diced
- 2 cloves of garlic, minced
- 2 cups Guinness
- 2 tablespoons tomato paste

- 2 bay leaves
- 2 tablespoons Worcestershire sauce
- 2 cups chicken broth
- 2 tablespoons cornstarch
- Salt and pepper to taste

Instructions:
1. Preheat oven to 350°F.
2. Heat olive oil in a large skillet or Dutch oven over medium-high heat.
3. Add duck legs and brown on both sides.
4. Remove duck legs and set aside.
5. Add onions, carrots, and garlic to the skillet and cook until vegetables are softened.
6. Add Guinness, tomato paste, bay leaves, and Worcestershire sauce. Stir to combine.
7. Add duck legs back to the skillet, making sure they are submerged in the liquid.
8. Cover skillet with a tight-fitting lid and transfer to preheated oven. Bake for 1½ to 2 hours until duck legs are tender.
9. Remove from oven and transfer duck legs to a plate.
10. In a small bowl, mix together chicken broth and cornstarch.
11. Bring liquid from skillet to a boil and stir in cornstarch mixture. Simmer for 5 minutes.
12. Return duck legs to skillet and cook for an additional 5 minutes until sauce has thickened.
13. Serve hot with your favorite side dishes.

Nutrition information: Per Serving – Calories: 690, Fat: 46g, Protein: 48g, Carbohydrates: 15g, Fiber: 2g, Sodium: 458mg

37. Guinness Chocolate Tart

This Guinness Chocolate Tart is one of the most delicious desserts made with the most iconic Irish beer. It is the perfect make-ahead dessert for your St. Patrick's Day celebrations.
Serving: 8
Preparation Time: 10 minutes
Ready Time: 30 minutes

Ingredients:
- 12 ounces semi-sweet chocolate chips
- 1/4 cup unsalted butter, melted
- 7 tablespoons Guinness beer
- 2 tablespoons sugar
- Pinch of salt
- 2 large eggs, lightly beaten
- 1 9-inch (23 cm) tart shell

Instructions:
1. Preheat oven to 350°F (180°C).
2. In a medium bowl, combine the chocolate chips, melted butter, Guinness, sugar, and salt. Stir until completely blended.
3. Add the eggs and mix until incorporated.
4. Pour the chocolate mixture into the prepared tart shell.
5. Bake in preheated oven for 25 to 30 minutes, or until set.
6. Cool completely before serving.

Nutrition information:
Serving size: 1 slice
Calories: 380 kcal
Fat: 21g
Carbohydrates: 39g
Protein: 6g
Sodium: 140mg

38. Guinness Beer Cheese Soup

Enjoy the classic Irish beverage in a delicious beer cheese soup with a savory and creamy texture. This comforting soup is a fun twist on the classic beer dish.
Serving: 6
Preparation time: 10 minutes
Ready time: 40 minutes

Ingredients:
- 2 tablespoons butter

- 2 cloves garlic, minced
- 2 tablespoons all-purpose flour
- 1 cup Guinness stout beer
- 2 cups chicken stock
- 1 teaspoon Worcestershire sauce
- 1/4 teaspoon ground cayenne pepper
- 1/2 teaspoon dried oregano
- 2 cups shredded cheddar cheese
- 2 tablespoons chopped fresh parsley

Instructions:
1. In a large saucepan, melt the butter over medium heat. Add the garlic and cook, stirring occasionally, until fragrant, about 1 minute.
2. Add the flour and stir well to combine. Cook for 1 minute more.
3. Whisk in the Guinness, chicken stock, Worcestershire sauce, cayenne pepper, and oregano. Increase the heat to medium-high and bring to a boil. Reduce the heat to low and simmer for 10 minutes, stirring occasionally.
4. Gradually stir in the cheese until melted. Taste and adjust the seasoning as desired.
5. Ladle the soup into bowls and garnish with the chopped parsley.

Nutrition information: 200 calories, 11 g fat, 12 g carbohydrates, 9 g protein

39. Guinness Chocolate Fondue

Refreshing and decadent, Guinness Chocolate Fondue is a delicious Irish-inspired treat that's perfect for any occasion. Impress your guests with this unusual twist on traditional chocolate fondue.
Serving: Serves 4-6
Preparation Time: 10 minutes
Ready Time: 10 minutes

Ingredients:
- 1/2 cup Guinness
- 2 (12 oz) semi-sweet chocolate chips
- 2 tablespoons Irish whiskey

- 1 tablespoon whipping cream
- 1 teaspoon cornstarch

Instructions:
1. In a medium saucepan over medium heat, combine Guinness with chocolate chips and Irish whiskey. Cook, stirring occasionally, until chocolate has melted.
2. In a small bowl, mix together whipping cream and cornstarch until smooth.
3. Slowly pour into the chocolate mixture, stirring constantly, and cook until the mixture thickens, about 5 minutes.
4. Serve warm with fruits, cookies, or your favorite desserts.

Nutrition information:
Serving Size: 1/4 cup
Calories: 164
Carbohydrates: 17.5 g (sugars 15.7 g)
Fat: 8.7 g
Protein: 2 g

40. Guinness Braised Chicken Thighs

Guinness Braised Chicken Thighs are a delicious way to add a unique flavor to chicken. The rich flavors of dark beer, bacon, onion, garlic, and spices combine for a delicious flavor that is sure to please.
Serving: 8
Preparation Time: 15 minutes
Ready Time: 45 minutes

Ingredients:
- 8 boneless skinless chicken thighs
- 2 tablespoons olive oil
- 2 slices bacon, diced
- 1 large onion, diced
- 1 clove garlic, minced
- 1 bottle Guinness Beer
- 1 tablespoon fresh sage, chopped
- 1 tablespoon fresh oregano, chopped

- 1 tablespoon fresh thyme, chopped
- 1 teaspoon sea salt
- 1 teaspoon freshly cracked black pepper
- 2 tablespoons balsamic vinegar

Instructions:
1. Preheat oven to 375 degrees.
2. Heat oil in an oven safe skillet over medium-high heat.
3. Add in the bacon and onion, cook until bacon is crisp and onion is translucent, about 8 minutes.
4. Add garlic and stir for 1 minute.
5. Add chicken thighs to the skillet and cook an additional 3 minutes.
6. Add Guinness beer to the skillet and bring to a simmer.
7. Add sage, oregano, thyme, salt, and pepper, and stir to combine.
8. Place skillet in preheated oven for 30 minutes.
9. Remove from oven and add balsamic vinegar, stirring to combine.
10. Serve.

Nutrition information: per serving – 310 calories, 19g fat, 6g saturated fat, 6g carbohydrates, 1g fiber, 28g protein

41. Guinness Chocolate Éclairs

Guinness Chocolate Éclairs are a delicious combination of sweet pastry cream and chocolate swirled with a hint of Guinness. Combining two sweet favorites, these éclairs are a delicious treat for any occasion.
Serving: 6
Preparation time: 40 minutes
Ready time: 1 hour

Ingredients:
- 1 cup (130g) all-purpose flour
- 1/2 teaspoon (3g) salt
- 1/2 cup (120g) butter
- 1 cup (240ml) water
- 4 large (200g) eggs
- 4 ounces (120ml) Guinness beer
- 8 ounces (225g) bittersweet chocolate, melted

- 8 ounces (225g) heavy cream

Instructions:
1. Preheat the oven to 400 F (205 C). Line two baking sheets with parchment paper.
2. In a medium bowl, whisk together the flour, salt, butter, water, eggs, and Guinness.
3. Using a spoon, drop the batter into 6 mounds on the prepared baking sheets.
4. Bake for 25 minutes, or until golden brown.
5. Let cool completely and remove from the baking sheet.
6. In a medium bowl, whip heavy cream until stiff peaks form.
7. Split the éclairs in half and fill with the whipped cream.
8. Drizzle the melted chocolate over the top.
9. Serve immediately or refrigerate until ready to serve.

Nutrition information:
Calories: 350, Fat: 22g, Saturated Fat: 13g, Cholesterol: 115mg, Sodium: 162mg, Carbohydrates: 30g, Fiber: 1g, Sugar: 16g, Protein: 6g

42. Guinness Braised Beef Brisket

Enjoy rich and comforting Guinness Braised Beef Brisket! This slow-cooking classic is packed with flavor from Guinness beer and onions, and made oh-so-tender when simmered in beef broth.
Serving: 4-6
Preparation Time: 15 minutes
Ready Time: 2 hours, 45 minutes

Ingredients:
- 2 tablespoons olive oil
- 4 pound beef brisket
- 2 onions, diced
- 4 cloves garlic, minced
- 2 tablespoons all-purpose flour
- 1 tablespoon dark brown sugar
- 1 (14.9 ounces) can Guinness beer
- 2 cups beef broth

- 2 bay leaves
- 2 tablespoons Worcestershire sauce
- Salt, as needed
- Pepper, as needed

Instructions:
1. Heat the olive oil in a large Dutch oven over medium-high heat, until shimmering.
2. Add the brisket and cook for 8-10 minutes, turning to ensure it browns evenly.
3. Reduce the heat to medium and add the onions and garlic, cooking until the onions are softened and lightly browned.
4. Add the flour and brown sugar, stirring to combine and cook for 2 minutes.
5. Slowly pour in the Guinness, stirring continuously to ensure it is completely incorporated.
6. Pour in the beef broth, bay leaves, and Worcestershire sauce and turn the heat to low.
7. Simmer for 2 hours, or until the brisket is fork-tender.
8. Once cooked, remove the brisket from the pot and season to taste with salt and pepper.
9. Slice and serve with cooked onions and pot juices.

Nutrition information: Per serving: 400 calories, 28g fat, 2g carbohydrate, 30g protein.

43. Guinness Chocolate Pecan Pie

This delicious and unique recipe combines the flavors of Guinness Beer with silky chocolate, crunchy pecans, and a flaky crust to create an indulgent and irresistible Guinness Chocolate Pecan Pie.
Serving: 8-10
Preparation Time: 25 minutes
Ready Time: 2 1/2 hours

Ingredients:
- 1 9-inch unbaked pie crust
- 2 tablespoons butter

- 2/3 cup light brown sugar, packed
- 1/2 teaspoon ground cinnamon
- 2/3 cup Golden syrup
- 3/4 cup Guinness
- 3 large eggs, lightly beaten
- 3/4 cup chopped pecans
- 1/2 cup semi-sweet chocolate chips

Instructions:
1. Preheat oven to 350°F (175°C).
2. Melt butter in a medium saucepan over medium heat. Add brown sugar, cinnamon and Golden syrup and stir until combined.
3. Stir in Guinness and bring to a simmer. Simmer for 4 minutes, stirring occasionally.
4. Remove from heat and let cool for 5 minutes.
5. In a medium bowl, whisk together eggs and pecans.
6. Gradually add cooled Guinness mixture, whisking constantly until combined.
7. Pour into prepared pie crust. Sprinkle with chocolate chips.
8. Bake for 40-45 minutes, or until a knife inserted in the center of the pie comes out clean.
9. Let cool completely before serving. Enjoy!

Nutrition information: Calories: 324 Fat: 14.5g Saturated Fat 5.1g Cholesterol 52mg Sodium 133mg Carbohydrate 35.8g Fiber 1.5g Protein 3.3g Sugars 11.7g

44. Guinness Beef Tacos

These tasty Guinness Beef Tacos are filled with well-seasoned and tender pieces of beef cooked in a rich Guinness marinade. They are full of flavor and a great meal for any Mexican-inspired night.
Serving: Makes 8 tacos
Preparation time: 10 minutes
Ready time: 40 minutes

Ingredients:
- 2 cloves garlic, minced

- 2 tablespoons olive oil
- ½ cup Guinness beer
- 1 teaspoon Worcestershire sauce
- 1 teaspoon dried oregano
- 1 teaspoon ground cumin
- 1 teaspoon smoked paprika
- Salt and pepper to taste
- 1 pound freshly ground beef
- 8 taco shells
- 1 cup cheddar cheese, grated
- 1 cup salsa
- 1 cup sour cream
- Chopped cilantro for garnish
- Lettuce, chopped onions, and tomatoes for garnish (optional)

Instructions:
1. In a large skillet over medium heat, sauté the garlic in the olive oil for 2 minutes.
2. Add in Guinness beer, Worcestershire sauce, oregano, cumin, paprika, salt, and pepper. Simmer for 10 minutes.
3. Add the ground beef and cook for 6-8 minutes, stirring often, until the beef is cooked through.
4. Place the taco shells on a baking sheet and fill each shell with the Guinness beef mixture. Top with cheese.
5. Place in the oven and broil on high for 2-3 minutes, until the cheese is melted.
6. Remove from the oven and top with lettuce, salsa, sour cream, cilantro, and any other toppings you desire. Serve immediately.

Nutrition information: Per serving (based on 8 servings): Total Calories: 375, Total Fat: 24g, Saturated Fat: 11g, Trans Fat: 0g, Cholesterol: 58mg, Sodium: 582mg, Total Carbohydrates: 19g, Dietary Fiber: 2g, Total Sugars: 5g, Protein: 17g.

45. Guinness Chocolate Martini

Enjoy the perfect combination of two classic indulgences—chocolate and a martini—with this delicious Guinness Chocolate Martini recipe.

Serving: Serves 1
Preparation Time: 5 minutes
Ready Time: 5 minutes

Ingredients:
- 2 ounces Baileys Irish Cream
- 1 ounce vodka
- 1 ounce Guinness Original
- 2 teaspoons chocolate sauce

Instructions:
1. Rim a martini glass with chocolate sauce.
2. In a shaker filled with ice, add Baileys Irish Cream, vodka, Guinness Original, and chocolate sauce.
3. Shake for 20-30 seconds.
4. Strain into the prepared martini glass.

Nutrition information:
Calories: 199
Total Fat: 0.2g
Carbohydrate: 23.5g
Protein: 0.2g

46. Guinness Glazed Ham

Start your next festive gathering with this classic Guinness glazed ham, a combination of flavorful Ingredients such as Guinness beer, honey and orange that will surely be a hit with family and friends!
Serving: 6-8
Preparation Time: 10 minutes
Ready Time: 2 hours

Ingredients:
1 (8 to 9 pound) bone-in fully cooked ham
1 (12-ounce) can Guinness beer
1 1/2 cups brown sugar
1/2 cup honey
1/4 cup honey mustard

1/4 cup orange marmalade

Instructions:
1. Preheat the oven to 350°F. Place the ham on a roasting rack in a roasting pan.
2. In a small saucepan, bring the Guinness and brown sugar to a simmer over medium-high heat. Simmer for 5 minutes, then remove from the heat and whisk in the honey, mustard and marmalade.
3. Bake the ham for 30 minutes and brush it with the glaze. Continue baking until the glaze is caramelized and the internal temperature of the ham registers 140°F on an instant-read thermometer, about 1 hour.
4. Allow the ham to rest for 10 minutes, then carve and serve with accompaniments, if desired.

Nutrition information:
Calories: 340, Fat: 13.4g, Carbohydrates: 25.5g, Protein: 20.3g

47. Guinness Chocolate Biscotti

Guinness Chocolate Biscotti is a rich, crunchy, and delicious Italian-style cookie that combines the bold flavors of Guinness beer and chocolate. Serving: Makes about 18 biscotti. Preparation time: 15 minutes Ready time: 25 minutes

Ingredients:
2 cups all-purpose flour
1 teaspoon baking powder
1/4 teaspoon salt
3/4 cup granulated sugar
2 large eggs
3 tablespoons Guinness stout beer
3/4 cup semi-sweet chocolate chips
2 tablespoons butter, melted

Instructions:
1. Preheat the oven to 375 degrees before you begin baking.
2. In a medium bowl, whisk together the flour, baking powder, and salt.
3. In a large bowl, beat the sugar and eggs until pale and fluffy.

4. Beat in the Guinness beer, and then slowly mix in the dry Ingredients.

5. Fold in the chocolate chips and melted butter.

6. Roll the dough into a log shape and place it on a lined baking sheet. Bake for 15 minutes.

7. Lower the oven temperature to 350 degrees and bake for another 10 minutes.

8. Remove from the oven and let cool for 5 minutes. Slice the biscotti into 1/2-inch slices and place back on the baking sheet.

9. Bake for 8 to 10 minutes, until the biscotti are golden brown and slightly crispy.

10. Remove from the oven and let cool on a wire rack before serving.

Nutrition information: Serving Size: 1 biscotti, Calories: 105, Fat: 3 g, Sodium: 70 mg, Carbohydrates: 17 g, Protein: 2 g.

48. Guinness Beef Stir Fry

Guinness Beef Stir Fry is an easy and flavourful dinner dish that combines beef and fresh vegetables to create a quick and savoury dinner. It's easy to adapt and personalise to your tastes and is sure to be a family favourite.

Serving: 4 servings

Preparation time: 10 minutes

Ready time: 15 minutes

Ingredients:
- 1 pound lean beef, thinly sliced
- 2 cloves garlic, minced
- 2 tablespoons canola oil
- 1 onion, diced
- 2 carrots, sliced julienne
- 2 stalks celery, diced
- 1 bell pepper, diced
- 1 teaspoon ground ginger
- 1 teaspoon ground coriander
- 1 can Guinness Draught Beer
- 2 tablespoons low-sodium soy sauce
- 2 tablespoons honey

Instructions:
1. In a large skillet, heat the canola oil over medium-high heat.
2. Add the beef and sear for a few minutes until lightly browned. Then add the garlic, onion, carrots, celery and bell pepper, sautéing for an additional five minutes or until the vegetables are just tender crisp.
3. Add the ginger and coriander, stirring to combine.
4. Carefully pour in the can of Guinness, stirring to combine, and cook until the beer is completely absorbed.
5. Add the soy sauce and honey, stirring to combine. Cook for an additional minute or two.
6. Serve hot over cooked white or brown rice.

Nutrition information: per serving: Calories 360; fat 12g; protein 35g; carbs 24g; fiber 5g.

49. Guinness Chocolate Bread Pudding

Guinness Chocolate Bread Pudding is a decadent and flavorful treat perfect for any occasion. This rich pudding is made from a combination of Guinness Stout, bittersweet chocolate, and bread, giving it a delicious, one-of-a-kind flavor.
Serving: Serves 8
Preparation time: 15 minutes
Ready time: 2 hours, 30 minutes

Ingredients:
- 5 cups challah bread, cubed
- 4 tablespoons salted butter
- 3 tablespoons light brown sugar
- ½ teaspoon ground cinnamon
- 2 tablespoons cocoa powder
- 10 ounces bittersweet chocolate chips
- 3 large eggs
- 1 ½ teaspoons pure vanilla extract
- 12 ounces Guinness Stout
- 2 cups whole milk
- 1/2 cup granulated sugar

- Pinch of kosher salt

Instructions:
1. Preheat the oven to 350°F. Grease a 9-inch square baking dish.
2. In a medium bowl, toss together the bread cubes, butter, brown sugar, cinnamon, and cocoa powder. Transfer the mixture into the prepared baking dish and bake for 10 minutes until lightly golden.
3. In a medium saucepan, melt the bittersweet chocolate chips. Once melted, add the eggs and whisk until smooth. Stir in the vanilla extract, Guinness Stout, milk, sugar and salt.
4. Pour the liquid mixture over the bread cubes and gently press the bread into the liquid with a spoon. Bake for 40 minutes, or until the pudding is set and lightly browned.

Nutrition information: 550 calories, 20g fat, 83g carbs, 16g protein

50. Guinness Braised Pork Chops

This savory Guinness Braised Pork Chops recipe is a hearty and flavorful Irish-inspired dish. Blending the classic flavors of bacon, beef, Guinness Beer, and caramelized onions, this is the perfect ingredient for a cozy dinner.
Serving: 4
Preparation Time: 10 minutes
Ready Time: 1 hour 45 minutes

Ingredients:
- 4 bone-in pork chops
- 1 tablespoon olive oil
- 1/2 cup chopped bacon
- 1 large onion, sliced
- 2 cloves garlic, minced
- 2 tablespoons all-purpose flour
- 1 cup beef stock
- 1/2 cup Guinness beer, or other dark beer
- 2 teaspoons Worcestershire sauce
- 1/4 teaspoon dried thyme
- Salt and pepper to taste

Instructions:
1. Preheat oven to 350°F (175°C).
2. Heat olive oil in a large, oven-proof skillet over medium-high heat.
3. Add bacon and cook until crisp, about 5 minutes.
4. Add onion and garlic and cook until softened, about 5 minutes.
5. Sprinkle flour over vegetables and stir to combine.
6. Add beef stock, Guinness beer, Worcestershire sauce, and thyme. Bring to a simmer.
7. Season pork chops with salt and pepper and add to skillet.
8. Transfer skillet to preheated oven, and bake until pork chops are cooked through, about 1 hour and 30 minutes.
9. Serve warm with mashed potatoes.

Nutrition information:
Calories: 500kcal, Carbohydrates: 16g, Protein: 37g, Fat: 31g, Saturated Fat: 11g, Cholesterol: 106mg, Sodium: 450mg, Potassium: 658mg, Fiber: 1g, Sugar: 4g, Vitamin A: 130IU, Vitamin C: 3mg, Calcium: 56mg, Iron: 3.2mg

51. Guinness Chocolate Lava Cake

Guinness Chocolate Lava Cake is an incredibly delicious dessert that combines the taste of rich chocolate cake and creamy Guinness beer. This decadent treat is surprisingly easy to make and filled with rich flavors.
Serving: 4
Preparation Time: 15 Minutes
Ready Time: 45 Minutes

Ingredients:
- 1 cup semi-sweet chocolate chips
- ½ cup Guinness beer
- ¼ cup butter
- 5 tablespoons all-purpose flour
- 2 eggs
- 2 tablespoons granulated sugar

Instructions:
1. Preheat the oven to 375 degrees F.
2. Grease a muffin pan with a little bit of butter and set aside.
3. In a small saucepan, melt the chocolate chips and Guinness beer together until fully melted.
4. Add the butter and stir until fully incorporated.
5. Remove from heat and add the flour, eggs, and sugar, stirring until a thick batter forms.
6. Pour the batter into the muffin pan, filling each cavity ¾ way full.
7. Bake for 25 minutes until the cakes are puffed and slightly brown on the edges.
8. Let cool for 5 minutes before removing from the pan.

Nutrition information: (Per Serving)
Calories: 230, Fat: 14 g, Cholesterol: 62 mg, Sodium: 70 mg, Carbohydrates: 25 g, Protein: 5 g

52. Guinness Beef Sliders with Caramelized Onions

This quick and easy recipe for Guinness Beef Sliders with Caramelized Onions is a delicious way to make the most out of juicy beef patties and flavorful sweet caramelized onions. Perfect for an appetizer or main dish, this comforting take on sliders will be sure to please.
Serving: 8
Preparation Time: 15 minutes
Ready Time: 30 minutes

Ingredients:
• 2 tablespoons olive oil
• 2 large onions, sliced
• 2 tablespoons light brown sugar
• 1 12-ounce bottle of Guinness
• 1 pound lean ground beef
• 2 tablespoons Worcestershire sauce
• Salt and black pepper
• 8 small hamburger buns, such as Kings Hawaiian
• 8 slices of extra sharp white cheddar cheese

Instructions:

1. In a large non-stick sauté pan, heat olive oil over medium to high heat. Add onions and season with a pinch of salt and pepper. Cook for about 10-12 minutes, stirring occasionally, until onions are golden and caramelized. Add light brown sugar and cook for a few additional minutes.

2. Meanwhile, combine beef, Guinness and Worcestershire sauce in a large bowl. Season with salt and pepper and mix until fully combined. Form the mixture into 8 thin patties and season both sides with salt and pepper.

3. Heat an outdoor grill over medium-high heat. Place patties on the grill and cook for approximately 5 minutes on each side (flip at least once), or until beef is cooked through. Add cheese slices to each patty during the last few minutes of cooking.

4. Serve patties on buns topped with caramelized onions and a dab of your favorite condiment. Enjoy!

Nutrition information: Per Serving (1 slider) - Calories: 288.3; Total Fat: 11.8g; Cholesterol: 40.6mg; Sodium: 310.2mg; Total Carbohydrate: 25.6g; Protein: 15.7g

53. Guinness Chocolate Muffins

These Guinness Chocolate Muffins are deliciously moist and make a perfect snack or for dessert. They combine the flavors of Guinness and rich chocolate that are sure to satisfy the taste buds.
Serving: Makes 12 muffins
Preparation Time: 20 minutes
Ready Time: 35 minutes

Ingredients:
- ½ cup Guinness
- 1 cup all-purpose flour
- ½ cup cocoa powder
- 2 teaspoons baking powder
- 1 cup brown sugar
- 1 teaspoon salt
- 2 eggs

- ½ cup melted butter

Instructions:
1. Preheat oven to 375°F (190°C).
2. In a medium bowl, whisk together all-purpose flour, cocoa powder, baking powder, brown sugar, and salt.
3. In a separate bowl, combine Guinness with melted butter and whisk until blended.
4. Beat in eggs, one at a time, stirring until the mixture is smooth.
5. Slowly add the dry Ingredients in with the wet Ingredients and stir until everything is combined.
6. Grease 12 muffin cups or line with paper cupcake liners.
7. Spoon batter into muffin cups, filling about two-thirds full.
8. Bake in preheated oven for 18-20 minutes or until a toothpick comes out clean.
9. Allow to cool before serving.

Nutrition information:
- 213 calories
- 11 g fat
- 27 g carbohydrates
- 3 g protein

54. Guinness Beef Skewers

Guiness Beef Skewers are a savory and delicious twist on the classic kabob. Packed with plenty of hearty vegetables and marinated in tangy Guinness stout, these juicy beef skewers are sure to satisfy.
Serving: Serves 4
Preparation Time: 15 minutes
Ready Time: 2 hours

Ingredients:
-2 large beefsteak tomatoes, sliced
-1 large sweet onion, cut into 8 wedges
-1 red pepper, cut into 8 wedges
-1 zucchini, cut into 8 small chunks
-1/2 cup olive oil

-1/4 cup Guinness stout
-2 tablespoons balsamic vinegar
-2 garlic cloves, minced
-1 teaspoon dried oregano
-1/2 teaspoon dried thyme
-1/2 teaspoon kosher salt
-1/4 teaspoon freshly ground black pepper
-1 pound beef sirloin, cut into 1-inch cubes

Instructions:
1. In a large bowl, combine the tomatoes, onion, red pepper, and zucchini and set aside.
2. In a small bowl, whisk together the oil, Guinness, vinegar, garlic, oregano, thyme, salt, and pepper.
3. Divide the beef cubes between the vegetables in the large bowl and pour the marinade over the top. Gently mix everything together, making sure all the pieces are coated with the marinade. Cover the bowl and refrigerate for at least 2 hours, or overnight.
4. Preheat a grill or grill pan to medium-high heat. Thread the chunks of beef and vegetables onto skewers. Discard the excess marinade.
5. Place the skewers on the preheated grill. Grill for about 8 minutes, turning the skewers halfway through cooking, or until the beef is cooked to desired doneness. Serve immediately.

Nutrition information: Per serving: Calories: 433, Fat: 22g, Saturated fat: 4g, Trans fat: 0g, Cholesterol: 78mg, Sodium: 327mg, Carbohydrates: 13g, Fiber: 2g, Sugar: 7g, Protein: 40g

55. Guinness Chocolate Cheesecake Brownies

Guinness Chocolate Cheesecake Brownies feature a luscious chocolate brownie with a rich cream cheese filling, all topped with a creamy Guinness-infused ganache.
Serving: 12
Preparation time: 15 minutes
Ready time: 2 hours 25 minutes

Ingredients:

- 2 cans of Guinness stout beer
- 1 box of brownie mix
- 2 8-ounce packages of cream cheese
- 2 tablespoons of butter
- 2 tablespoons of flour
- 1/2 cup packed dark brown sugar
- 2 large eggs
- 1 1/2 cups semisweet chocolate chips
- 1/2 cup heavy cream

Instructions:
1. Preheat oven to 350°F and lightly grease an 11x7-inch baking pan.
2. In a medium saucepan, bring Guinness to low boil and let it reduce by half. This should take 10 to 15 minutes.
3. While Guinness is reducing, prepare the brownie mix according to box instructions and pour into prepared pan.
4. In a medium bowl, beat together the cream cheese, butter, flour, and brown sugar until smooth.
5. Add the eggs one at a time, mixing after each addition.
6. Once the Guinness is reduced, allow it to cool for several minutes.
7. Pour the cream cheese mixture over the top of the brownie mix, and spread evenly.
8. Drizzle cooled Guinness over cream cheese mixture and use a spoon or a spatula to gently swirl.
9. Bake for 25 to 30 minutes, until edges are lightly browned and cheesecake is set.
10. Allow the brownies to cool for 30 minutes before preparing the ganache.
11. In a medium bowl, mix together the chocolate chips and heavy cream until smooth.
12. Spread ganache evenly over brownies in pan and allow to cool for 1 hour before serving.

Nutrition information: Per serving (12 servings): Calories: 529; Total Fat: 25g; Saturated Fat: 14g; Cholesterol: 76mg; Sodium: 181mg; Carbohydrates: 67g; Fiber: 2.4g; Sugar: 50g; Protein: 8.4g.

56. Guinness Braised Turkey Legs

Guinness braised turkey legs are tender and succulent which are slow-cooked in a mixture of Guinness beer, vegetables, butter, and herbs. This is a great way to turn regular turkey legs into a delicious meal.
Serving: 4
Preparation Time: 15 minutes
Ready Time: 2½ hours

Ingredients:
4 turkey legs
2 tablespoons butter
1 large onion, chopped
3 cloves garlic, minced
1 teaspoon Italian seasoning
¼ teaspoon garlic powder
2 (14.9-ounce) bottles Guinness Stout
1 cup chicken broth
Salt and freshly ground black pepper

Instructions:
1. Preheat the oven to 350°F.
2. Melt the butter in a large ovenproof skillet over medium-high heat. Add the turkey legs and season with salt and pepper. Cook until they begin to brown, about 7 minutes.
3. Add the onion, garlic, Italian seasoning, and garlic powder. Cook for 3 minutes.
4. Stir in the Guinness and chicken broth. Bring to a simmer and then transfer the skillet to the oven.
5. Bake for 1½ to 2 hours, until the turkey legs are tender.

Nutrition information: Calories: 362 kcal, Carbohydrates: 8 g, Protein: 25 g, Fat: 19 g, Saturated Fat: 8 g, Cholesterol: 109 mg, Sodium: 338 mg, Potassium: 568 mg, Fiber: 1 g, Sugar: 2 g, Vitamin A: 208 IU, Vitamin C: 7 mg, Calcium: 22 mg, Iron: 2 mg

57. Guinness Chocolate Soufflé

This light, airy and delicious Guinness Chocolate Soufflé is the perfect way to end a meal. Rich in dark chocolate and with a hint of the malt and roasted barley flavor of Guinness, this dessert definitely hits the spot.

Serving: 12 servings
Preparation time: 10 minutes
Ready time: 55 minutes

Ingredients:
- 3/4 cup heavy cream
- 1/2 cup Guinness beer
- 1/2 cup sugar
- 4 large egg yolks
- 4 ounces bittersweet chocolate, finely chopped
- 4 egg whites
- 2 tablespoons powdered sugar

Instructions:
1. Preheat oven to 350 F. Grease several 10-ounce deep-dish individual ramekins or soufflé dishes with butter.
2. In a medium saucepan, combine cream and Guinness over medium heat. Heat until almost boiling.
3. In a separate bowl, whisk together the sugar and egg yolks until combined. Gradually whisk in the heated cream mixture until combined.
4. Place the chopped chocolate in a bowl and pour the egg mixture over it. Stir until the chocolate is melted and the mixture is smooth.
5. In a bowl, beat the egg whites until foamy. Slowly add the powdered sugar and continue to beat until stiff peaks form.
6. Gently fold the egg whites into the chocolate mixture. Pour the mixture into the prepared ramekins.
7. Bake for 45 to 55 minutes until puffed and lightly golden. Serve immediately.

Nutrition information: Per serving (1/12 of recipe): 285 calories, 18 g fat, 135 mg cholesterol, 24 g carbohydrate, 4 g fiber, 7 g protein, 160 mg sodium.

58. Guinness Braised Bratwurst

Guinness Braised Bratwurst is a savory and delicious dish that combines flavorful bratwurst with a rich Guinness gravy. The bratwursts are cooked low and slow in the gravy for maximum flavor and then served with potatoes or a fresh salad.

Serving: 4

Preparation Time: 15 minutes

Ready Time: 1 hour

Ingredients:
- 4 bratwurst
- 2 cups Guinness Stout
- 2 tablespoons butter
- 2 tablespoons olive oil
- 1 onion, diced
- 2 cloves garlic, minced
- 1 tablespoon Worcestershire sauce
- 2 tablespoons all-purpose flour
- 1 cup beef broth
- Salt and pepper, to taste

Instructions:
1. Preheat oven to 300°F.
2. In a large oven-safe skillet, melt butter with olive oil over medium heat.
3. Add in diced onion and bratwurst, cooking for 5-7 minutes until bratwurst is browned.
4. Add in garlic, Worcestershire sauce, and flour, cooking for an additional minute until fragrant.
5. Slowly pour in Guinness and beef broth, stirring until combined.
6. Reduce heat to low and simmer for 20 minutes, until gravy has thickened.
7. Transfer skillet to preheated oven and bake for 30 minutes.
8. Serve braised bratwurst and gravy over potatoes or a fresh salad.

Nutrition information:
Calories: 350, Fat: 18g, Carbohydrates: 4g, Protein: 28g, Sodium: 500mg

59. Guinness Chocolate Pots de Crème

Guinness Chocolate Pots de Crème is a creamy and smooth custard-like dessert made with Guinness beer, chocolate, and cream.
Serving: Makes 4 servings.
Preparation time: 10 minutes
Ready time: 10 minutes (plus 4-6 hours to chill)

Ingredients:
- 2 cups heavy cream
- 1 cup Guinness beer
- 1/2 cup sugar
- 1/2 teaspoon vanilla extract
- 8 ounces semi-sweet chocolate chips

Instructions:
1. In a medium saucepan, heat cream, beer, and sugar over medium heat, stirring occasionally.
2. When mixture is hot, add chocolate chips and stir until fully melted and smooth.
3. Remove mixture from heat and stir in vanilla extract.
4. Pour mixture into four ramekins and refrigerate for 4-6 hours (or overnight).

Nutrition information: Per serving:
- Calories 645
- Fat 44g
- Saturated fat 29g
- Cholesterol 112mg
- Sodium 45mg
- Carbohydrates 52g
- Fiber 3g
- Sugar 45g
- Protein 8g

60. Guinness Beef Tamales

Guinness Beef Tamales are a savory, hearty Mexican dish that are the perfect entrée for special occasions or just a flavorful meal anytime.
Serving: Makes 16 tamales
Preparation time: 1 hour
Ready time: 1 hour 30 minutes

Ingredients:
- 2 ½ cups beef broth
- 1 (11.2 ounce) can Guinness Draught
- 2 tablespoons olive oil
- 1 onion, diced
- 2 tablespoons minced garlic
- 1 ½ teaspoon chili powder
- 2 teaspoon ground cumin
- 1 teaspoon dried oregano
- 2 cups cooked and diced beef
- 1 (7 ounce) can green chiles
- 2 tablespoons masa harina
- 1 teaspoon salt
- 2 cups shredded Cheddar cheese
- 2 cups frozen corn
- 16 dried corn husks

Instructions:
1. In a large saucepan, heat beef broth, Guinness Draught, olive oil, onion, garlic, chili powder, cumin, and oregano over medium heat. Simmer for 15 minutes.
2. Add cooked beef, green chiles, masa harina, and salt and stir to combine. Simmer over low heat for 15 minutes.
3. Turn off heat and stir in cheese and corn. Let mixture cool for 15 minutes.
4. Soak corn husks in warm water for 10 minutes.
5. Place 2 tablespoons of the beef mixture in the middle of a soaked husk. Fold the husk in half and tie with a piece of string.
6. Place the tamales in a steamer basket above 2 inches of boiling water. Cover and steam for 40 minutes.
7. Let the tamales cool before serving.

Nutrition information: Per Serving: Calories: 162, Fat: 7g, Carbohydrates: 16g, Protein: 7g, Sodium: 331mg, Cholesterol: 18mg.

61. Guinness Chocolate Filled Donuts

Guinness Chocolate Filled Donuts are a delicious and unique fusion of two beloved treats — chocolate and donuts. These decadent donuts are easy to make and are perfect for a special occasion or just a fancy sweet treat to indulge in.
Serving: 12 donuts
Preparation time: 25 minutes
Ready time: 45 minutes

Ingredients:
-1/2 cup Guinness beer
-1/3 cup cocoa powder
-1/2 teaspoon sea salt
-1/2 teaspoon baking soda
-1/2 teaspoon ground cinnamon
-1/4 cup butter, melted
-1/2 cup sugar
-1 large egg
-1 teaspoon vanilla extract
-1 1/4 cup all-purpose flour
-1/4 cup chocolate chips
-Oil, for deep frying
-Powdered sugar, for garnish

Instructions:
1. In a medium bowl, whisk together the Guinness, cocoa powder, salt, baking soda, and cinnamon until smooth.
2. In a separate bowl, cream together the melted butter and sugar, until combined. Add in the egg and vanilla extract and mix until well incorporated.
3. Gradually add the wet Ingredients to the dry Ingredients and mix until completely combined.

4. Stir in the chocolate chips to the dough and mix until they are evenly distributed.

5. Refrigerate the dough for 30 minutes to allow it to firm up.

6. Heat oil in a medium-sized pot or deep fryer over medium heat, until it reaches 375 degrees Fahrenheit.

7. Take spoonfuls of the dough and form into doughnut shapes. Carefully place them in the hot oil and fry for 2-3 minutes, until golden brown.

8. Remove from the oil and place on a paper towel-lined plate. Sprinkle with powdered sugar, as desired. Enjoy warm.

Nutrition information:
Serving size: 1 donut
Calories: 235
Total fat: 9g
Saturated fat: 6g
Trans fat: 0g
Carbohydrates: 34g
Sugar: 19g
Protein: 4g

62. Guinness Braised Rabbit

This classic and comforting dish pairs tender rabbit meat cooked in a rich and slightly bitter Guinness and bacon sauce. It's a great meal to make on a colder day.
Serving: 6
Preparation time: 15 minutes
Ready time: 1 hour

Ingredients:
- 1 (3- 4 lb) whole rabbit, cut into 8 pieces
- 2 tablespoons olive oil
- 4 ounces thick cut bacon, finely chopped
- 2 cups diced onion
- 4 cloves garlic, minced
- 1 tablespoon chopped fresh thyme
- 2 tablespoons tomato paste

- 2 tablespoons all-purpose flour
- 1/2 teaspoon ground mustard
- 2 (12-ounce) bottles of Guinness
- 1 cup chicken stock
- Salt and freshly ground black pepper

Instructions:
1. Preheat oven to 400°F.
2. Heat the olive oil in a large Dutch oven over medium heat. Add bacon and cook until lightly browned.
3. Add the onion and garlic and cook until softened, about 5 minutes. Stir in the thyme, tomato paste, flour, and ground mustard.
4. Pour in the Guinness and chicken stock and bring to a simmer.
5. Add the rabbit pieces, cover, and transfer to the oven for 40 minutes.
6. Remove the rabbit from the pan and set aside. Simmer the sauce over medium heat to reduce and thicken, about 10 minutes.
7. Return the rabbit pieces to the pan and toss to coat. Serve warm.

Nutrition information: Calories: 455; Protein: 29.3g; Fat: 19.3g; Carbohydrate: 20.3g; Fiber: 1.1g; Sodium: 845mg

63. Guinness Chocolate Whoopie Pies

Guinness Chocolate Whoopie Pies are soft, fudgy chocolate cakes sandwiched around a light, creamy filling. This indulgent chocolate treat makes a delicious dessert for any celebration.
Serving: 12
Preparation Time: 15 minutes
Ready Time: 1 hour

Ingredients:
• 2 cups all-purpose flour
• 1 cup cocoa powder
• 1½ teaspoon baking powder
• ½ teaspoon baking soda
• ½ cup unsalted butter, at room temperature
• ¾ cup granulated sugar
• 1 cup low-fat buttermilk

- 2 eggs
- 1 teaspoon vanilla extract
- 2 cups Guinness beer
- 2 cups whipped cream

Instructions:
1. Preheat oven to 350 degrees F and line a baking sheet with parchment paper.
2. In a medium bowl, whisk together flour, cocoa powder, baking powder and baking soda. Add butter and sugar and mix until well combined.
3. In a separate bowl, combine buttermilk, eggs, vanilla extract and Guinness beer and mix until smooth.
4. Slowly add wet Ingredients to dry Ingredients and mix until smooth.
5. Using a small ice cream scoop, drop batter onto prepared baking sheet, about 1-inch apart.
6. Bake for 10-12 minutes, or until a toothpick inserted into the center comes out clean. Let cool completely on a wire rack.
7. To assemble the pies, place a dollop of whipped cream on top of one cookie, then top with another and press lightly to create a sandwich.

Nutrition information: per serving:
Calories: 180, Total Fat: 6 g, Saturated Fat: 4 g, Cholesterol: 28 mg, Sodium: 85 mg, Carbohydrates: 28 g, Fiber: 2 g, Sugar: 11 g, Protein: 3 g.

64. Guinness Beer Can Chicken

Guinness Beer Can Chicken is a classic American dish that infuses succulent and juicy roasted chicken with a delicious hint of beer flavor. The beer keeps the chicken moist and flavors the meat, making it an incredibly tender dish.
Serving: 4
Preparation time: 20 minutes
Ready time: 1 hour, 30 minutes

Ingredients:
-1 can of Guinness beer
-1 whole chicken

-2 tablespoons of olive oil
-1 tablespoon of garlic powder
-1 tablespoon of smoked paprika
-2 teaspoons of onion powder
-1 teaspoon of black pepper
-1 teaspoon of kosher salt
-1 lemon

Instructions:
1. Preheat your oven to 375 degrees.
2. Rinse off the chicken in cold water and pat it dry.
3. Use the olive oil to rub all over the chicken, ensuring it is fully coated.
4. In a small bowl combine the garlic powder, smoked paprika, onion powder, black pepper, and salt together.
5. Sprinkle the seasoning mixture over the chicken and massage it into the skin.
6. Take a can of Guinness and carefully insert the chicken over the can.
7. Place the chicken in the oven and bake for 1 hour and 15 minutes, or until the skin is golden brown and crispy.
8. Once done baking, carefully remove the beer can from the chicken.
9. Squeeze a lemon over the chicken to add additional flavor.
10. Slice the Guinness Beer Can Chicken and serve.

Nutrition information:
Calories: 480
Total Fat: 30 g
Saturated Fat: 7 g
Carbohydrates: 4 g
Protein: 34 g
Cholesterol: 117 mg
Sodium: 836 mg
Sugar: 2 g

65. Guinness Chocolate Éclair Cake

Guinness Chocolate Éclair Cake is a decadent, rich, and creamy chocolate dessert. Perfect for any dinner parties or special events.
Serving: 6-8 Preparation Time: 45 minutes Ready Time: 5 hours

Ingredients:
- 2 tablespoons of butter
- 1 (3.5 ounce) box of instant vanilla pudding mix
- 2 cups of heavy cream
- 1 (12 ounce) can of Guinness Extra Stout beer
- 1 (16 ounce) package of frozen whipped topping, thawed
- 2 (4 ounce) packages of sugar-free chocolate instant pudding mix
- 2 sheets of frozen puff pastry, thawed
- 2 cups of semi-sweet chocolate chips

Instructions:
1. Preheat oven to 375 degrees F. Grease a 9x13 inch baking pan with butter.
2. In a medium bowl, mix together the instant vanilla pudding mix, heavy cream, and the Guinness beer. Beat until combined. Pour the mixture into the prepared baking pan and spread evenly.
3. Place the puff pastry sheets on top of the pudding mixture. Bake for 25 minutes.
4. In a medium bowl, mix together the thawed whipped topping, the chocolate instant pudding mix, and the semi-sweet chocolate chips. Spread the mixture on top of the puff pastry.
5. Refrigerate for at least four hours before serving.

Nutrition information (per serving): 411 calories, 18.2g fat, 56.2g carbohydrates, and 7.2g protein.

66. Guinness Braised Oxtail

Guinness Braised Oxtail is a delicious and flavorful dish that combines oxtail with the rich flavor of Guinness beer. It takes some time but is sure to add a unique taste to your meal. Serving: 4 Preparation Time: 10 minutes Ready Time: 4 hours

Ingredients:
- 2.5 pounds of oxtail
- 2 tablespoon olive oil
- 2 medium onions, diced

- 1 garlic bulb, minced
- 2 tablespoons tomato paste
- 2 tablespoons brown sugar
- 1 tablespoon thyme
- 2 bay leaves
- 2 cups of Guinness beer
- 2 cups beef broth
- 1 teaspoon Kosher salt
- 1 teaspoon ground black pepper

Instructions:
1. Heat olive oil in a large stockpot over medium heat. Add the oxtail pieces and brown for 8-10 minutes before stirring in the onions and garlic. Cook for an additional 5 minutes.
2. Stir in tomato paste, brown sugar, thyme and bay leaves. Cook for a couple of more minutes before adding the Guinness, beef broth, salt, and pepper.
3. Reduce heat to low and simmer, covered, for 4 hours or until oxtail is fork tender and sauce is thick and flavorful.
4. Serve oxtail in shallow bowls and spoon sauce over the top. Serve with crusty bread if desired.

Nutrition information (per serving): Calories: 435; Carbohydrates: 10g; Protein: 24g; Fat: 29g; Saturated Fat: 11g; Sodium: 1400mg; Cholesterol: 173mg.

67. Guinness Chocolate Bread

This Guinness Chocolate Bread is a unique twist on a classic dessert, combining two favorites into one delicious treat that everyone will love. With its rich dark chocolate and subtle notes of Guinness, this bread is sure to be a hit with all!
Serving: 2 loaves
Preparation time: 10 mins
Ready time: 70 mins

Ingredients:
• 2 cups all-purpose flour

- 1 teaspoon baking powder
- 1/2 teaspoon baking soda
- 1/4 teaspoon salt
- 2 tablespoons cocoa powder
- 1/2 cup semisweet chocolate chips
- 1/4 cup dark brown sugar
- 2 tablespoons melted butter
- 1 can Guinness draught
- 2 large eggs
- 1 teaspoon vanilla extract

Instructions:
1. Preheat oven to 375°F. Grease and flour two 9×5 inch loaf pans.
2. In a medium bowl, whisk together flour, baking powder, baking soda, salt, cocoa powder, and chocolate chips.
3. In a separate bowl, cream together brown sugar, butter, and Guinness.
4. Beat in eggs one at a time, then stir in vanilla.
5. Gradually mix the wet Ingredients into the dry ones until just combined.
6. Divide batter evenly between the two pans and bake for 60-65 minutes, or until a toothpick inserted into the center comes out clean and the bread is firm to the touch.
7. Allow the loaves to cool before removing from the pans.

Nutrition information:
- Calories: 258.2
- Fat: 8.5g
- Saturated Fat: 5.1g
- Carbohydrates: 37.2g
- Fiber: 1.2g
- Protein: 4.8g

68. Guinness Beef Empanadas

These Guinness Beef Empanadas are filled with beef, carrots, onion, and garlic and then sealed in a flaky crust for a hearty hand pie you won't be able to resist.
Serving: 8-10 empanadas

Preparation Time: 40 minutes
Ready Time: 1 hour and 30 minutes

Ingredients:
For the crust:
- 2.5 cups all-purpose flour
- 1 teaspoon salt
- 1/2 cup Guinness
- 1 cup cold unsalted butter, diced

For the filling:
- 1.5 pounds ground beef
- 2 cloves of garlic, minced
- 1/2 onion, chopped
- 1 cup baby carrots, chopped
- 1 teaspoon cumin
- 2 tablespoons Guinness
- Salt and pepper to taste

Instructions:
1. Preheat the oven to 350°F and line a baking sheet with parchment paper.
2. Place the flour and salt in a large bowl. Pour the Guinness and the butter over the flour mixture and use a pastry blender or your hands to mix the Ingredients together until a dough is formed. Wrap the dough in plastic and place it in the refrigerator for 20 minutes.
3. Meanwhile, place the ground beef in a large skillet over medium heat and cook until no longer pink. Add the garlic, onion, and carrots, and cook until softened. Add the cumin, Guinness, salt, and pepper and mix until well combined.
4. Take the dough from the refrigerator and roll it out into a large circle on a lightly floured surface. Cut the dough into 8-10 large circles (using a large biscuit cutter or the rim of a large cup). Place 1-2 tablespoons of filling onto the center of each circle, then dab the edges with warm water and fold them in half to make a half-moon shape. Seal the edges with a fork and place the empanadas onto the prepared baking sheet.
5. Bake in the preheated oven for 25-30 minutes, or until golden brown. Remove from oven and let cool before serving.

Nutrition information: Servings: 8-10 | 400 Calories per serving | Total Fat: 18.2g | Saturated Fat: 7.6 g | Cholesterol: 69.3 mg |

Sodium: 273.3 mg | Total Carbohydrate: 33.7g | Dietary Fiber: 2.1 g | Sugars: 0.9 g | Protein: 15.9 g

69. Guinness Chocolate Brioche

This delicious and unique recipe pairs the bold and rich notes of Guinness with creamy and sweet chocolate. The result is a sophisticated French-style breakfast bread perfect for impressing guests.
Serving: 10-12 people
Preparation time: 2 hours 20 minutes
Ready time: 2 hours 55 minutes

Ingredients:
- 2 ½ cups all-purpose flour
- ¼ tsp salt
- ¼ cup packed dark-brown sugar
- 1 pkg active dry yeast
- 4 Tbsp unsalted butter, softened
- ¼ cup whole milk
- 6 ounces dark chocolate, coarsely chopped
- 12 ounce Guinness

Instructions:
1. Combine the all-purpose flour, salt, brown sugar, and active dry yeast in the large bowl of a stand mixer fitted with the dough hook.
2. Add in the softened butter and mix on low to combine.
3. Turn the mixer to medium-low and slowly add in the Guinness and the whole milk until a shaggy dough forms.
4. Increase the speed of the mixer to medium and knead until the dough is smooth and elastic, about 5 minutes.
5. Add in the chopped dark chocolate and continue kneading for an additional 5 minutes, until the chocolate is evenly distributed throughout the dough.
6. Turn the dough out onto a lightly floured surface and shape it into a ball.
7. Grease a large bowl with butter, place the dough in the bowl, and cover with plastic wrap.

8. Let the dough rise at room temperature for 1½ hours; the dough should double in size.
9. Grease a 9x5-inch baking pan.
10. Turn the dough out onto a lightly floured surface. Cut the dough into 10-12 equal pieces and shape into rounds.
11. Place the rounds in the prepared pan. Cover the pan with plastic wrap and let the rolls rise at room temperature until they have doubled in size, about 45 minutes.
12. Preheat the oven to 375°F.
13. Bake for 25 minutes, until the rolls are golden brown.
14. Let cool in the pan for 10 minutes before serving.

Nutrition information:
Each roll contains about 230 calories, 8 grams of fat, 40 grams of carbohydrates, 1 gram of fiber, 4 grams of protein, and 140 milligrams of sodium.

70. Guinness Braised Quail

Guinness Braised Quail is a sumptuous dish with succulent quail braised in a rich and flavorful Guinness gravy.
Serving: 4
Preparation time: 30 minutes
Ready time: 1 hour

Ingredients:
• 4 quail
• ¼ cup olive oil
• 2 cloves of garlic, minced
• 1 tsp fresh rosemary
• 1 tbsp honey
• 1 cup Guinness beer
• 2 tbsp honey mustard
• 1 cup chicken broth
• Salt and pepper to taste

Instructions:
1. Preheat the oven to 375°F.

2. Heat the olive oil in large oven-safe frying pan over medium heat.
3. Add the garlic and rosemary to the pan and stir for 1 minute.
4. Add the quail and season with salt and pepper.
5. Cook until the quail are lightly browned, about 5 minutes.
6. Add the honey, Guinness beer, honey mustard, and chicken broth and bring to a boil.
7. Reduce the heat to low and cover the pan.
8. Simmer for 15 minutes or until the quail are cooked through.
9. Turn off the heat and transfer the pan to the preheated oven.
10. Bake for 30 minutes, stirring occasionally.
11. Serve with wild rice or potatoes.

Nutrition information (per serving): Calories: 367; Fat: 14.3g; Carbs: 11.0g; Protein: 20.1g; Sodium: 845mg; Sugar: 7.0g

71. Guinness Chocolate Caramel Slice

Guinness Chocolate Caramel Slice is a luscious layer of silky caramel, crunchy biscuit base and a smooth combination of dark chocolate and Guinness.
Serving: 12
Preparation time: 10 Minutes
Ready time: 2 Hours

Ingredients:
 40g butter, 25g brown sugar, 25g caster sugar, 175g plain sweet biscuit crumbs, 1/4 tsp ground ginger, 1/2 tsp cinnamon, 115g dried figs,60ml tepid Guinness, 70g dark choc chips, 392g tin condensed milk

Instructions:
1. Pre-heat oven to 160°C (320°F) and line a 20 cm (8 inch) square tin with baking paper.
2. In a medium bowl, cream butter and both sugars together until light and fluffy.
3. Add biscuit crumbs, ground ginger and cinnamon to the butter and sugar mixture and combine well.
4. Place the biscuit mixture into the prepared tin and pat down firmly to cover the base.

5. Bake for 10 minutes until golden brown and set aside to cool.

6. In a high-speed blender, place the figs and Guinness and blend until smooth.

7. Place the chocolate chips into a glass bowl and heat in the microwave for 15 second intervals, stirring until melted.

8. Place the condensed milk into a medium saucepan on medium-high heat. Stir continuously until it thickens and the bubbles become larger.

9. Add the figs and Guinness mixture to the condensed milk and stir until combined.

10. Pour the caramel mixture on top of the cooled biscuit base and spread evenly.

11. Sprinkle the melted chocolate onto the caramel topping and using an angled spatula spread the chocolate evenly.

12. Allow to cool completely in the tin before cutting into 12 slices.

Nutrition information: Per slice: Calories – 340, Total Fat – 11g, Saturated Fat – 5g, Protein – 5g, Carbohydrates – 51g, Sugar – 40g, Sodium – 95mg.

72. Guinness BBQ Pork Ribs

Guinness BBQ Pork Ribs are a savory and flavor-packed entrée that will keep your guests coming back for more. With a hint of malty Guinness flavor, these barbecue ribs are succulent and easy to make.

Serving: 4

Preparation Time: 10 minutes

Ready Time: 2 ½ hours

Ingredients:
- 2 racks baby back pork ribs
- 2 tablespoons olive oil
- 2 tablespoons garlic, minced
- 1 teaspoon kosher salt
- 1 teaspoon black pepper
- 1 cup Guinness beer
- 1 cup BBQ sauce

Instructions:

1. Preheat oven to 375°F.
2. Place the ribs on a baking sheet lined with foil.
3. Drizzle the ribs with oil, then rub the garlic, salt, and pepper onto both sides of the ribs.
4. Pour the Guinness onto the baking sheet.
5. Wrap the ribs in foil, trapping some of the beer inside the packet.
6. Bake in the preheated oven for 2 hours.
7. Carefully open the packet and spread the BBQ sauce over the ribs.
8. Bake for an additional 30 minutes.
9. Serve and enjoy!

Nutrition information: Nutritional values per serving: Calories: 795, Total Fat: 50.5g, Saturated Fat: 18.8g, Cholesterol: 177mg, Sodium: 902mg, Carbohydrates: 24.5g, Fiber: 0.5g, Sugar: 11.2g, Protein: 54.7g

73. Guinness Chocolate Meringue Pie

This delicious Guinness Chocolate Meringue Pie is a unique twist on the classic dessert favorite. It combines the richness of dark chocolate with Irish cream and the creamy texture of meringue to create a winning combination! It is sure to be a hit at any dinner party.
Serving: 8
Preparation Time: 20 minutes
Ready Time: 2 hours

Ingredients:
- 1/2 cup (120 ml) Guinness beer
- 1/2 cup (125 ml) Irish cream
- 2 (4.4 ounces/125 g) dark chocolate bars, chopped
- 9 ounces (250 g) ready-made chocolate pastry
- 3 egg whites, room temperature
- Pinch of salt
- 1/3 cup (75 g) granulated sugar

Instructions:
1. Preheat oven to 350°F (175°C).
2. Line an 8-inch (20 cm) pie pan with ready-made pastry.

3. In a medium bowl, whisk together Guinness and Irish cream.
4. Stir in chopped chocolate until completely melted.
5. Pour mixture into prepared pastry crust.
6. In a stand mixer, whisk egg whites with salt until soft peaks form.
7. Gradually add sugar until stiff peaks form.
8. Spread meringue over chocolate mixture in the pie pan.
9. Bake for 30 minutes, or until golden brown.
10. Allow to cool before serving.

Nutrition information: Per serving: Approximately 180 kcal, 6.6 g fat, 22.6 g carbs, 1.9 g fibre, 9.3 g protein.

74. Guinness Braised Sausages

Enjoy a taste of Irish pub fare with this easy Guinness braised sausage recipe. It's great for a midweek dinner or as an appetizer.
Serving: 6
Preparation time: 10 minutes
Ready time: 30 minutes

Ingredients:
- 2 tablespoons vegetable oil
- 2 cloves garlic, minced
- 6 links of your favorite sausage
- 1/2 onion, diced
- 1/2 cup Guinness
- 1 1/2 cups chicken broth
- 1 tablespoon dried parsley

Instructions:
1. Heat the oil in a large skillet over medium-high heat. Add the garlic and sauté until fragrant, about 2 minutes.
2. Add the sausage links and cook until golden brown on all sides, about 10 minutes.
3. Reduce the heat to medium and add the diced onion. Sauté until the onion is softened, about 5 minutes.

4. Pour in the Guinness and chicken broth and add the dried parsley. Bring the mixture to a simmer, then reduce the heat to low and cover the skillet.
5. Simmer the sausages, covered, for 15 minutes.
6. Serve hot with your favorite sides.

Nutrition information:
Calories: 263, Total Fat: 16 g, Saturated Fat: 6 g, Cholesterol: 37 mg, Sodium: 626 mg, Total Carbohydrate: 8 g, Protein: 18 g

75. Guinness Chocolate Tiramisu

This decadent Guinness Chocolate Tiramisu is a dessert take on the classic Italian Tiramisu pastry, where Ladyfinger cookies are soaked in coffee and layered with a creamy mascarpone mixture, flavored with cocoa and Guinness beer.
Serving: 6
Preparation Time: 10 minutes
Ready Time: 2 hours

Ingredients:
-30 Ladyfinger cookies
-568ml Guinness Draught Beer
- 2 tablespoons instant espresso powder
-3 tablespoons granulated sugar
-3 large eggs
-453g mascarpone cheese
-50g dark chocolate chips
-1/4 cup cocoa powder

Instructions:
1. Preheat oven to 190°C. Line a baking sheet with parchment paper.
2. Spread the Ladyfinger cookies on the baking sheet, and bake for 8 minutes until lightly golden.
3. In a medium bowl, whisk together Guinness beer, espresso powder, and sugar until espresso is completely dissolved.
4. In a medium bowl, whisk together eggs and mascarpone cheese until light and fluffy.

5. Add dark chocolate chips and cocoa powder to the Guinness mixture and whisk until fully incorporated.
6. Slowly add the Guinness mixture to the mascarpone mixture and mix until fully combined.
7. Dip the Ladyfingers into the Guinness mixture and layer them in a 9-inch square baking dish.
8. Layer half the mascarpone mixture over the cookies, followed by the remaining cookies and remaining mascarpone mixture.
9. Refrigerate the Tiramisu for at least two hours before serving.

Nutrition information: Calories: 525, Total Fat: 32g, Saturated Fat: 17g, Cholesterol: 172mg, Sodium: 253mg, Carbohydrates: 42.g, Fiber: 1g, Sugar: 26g, Protein: 11g

76. Guinness Beef Enchiladas

Guinness Beef Enchiladas are a delicious and unique spin on traditional Mexican enchiladas. The filling is made with tasty ground beef, beans, and Guinness Stout that is simmered together creating a creamy filling bursting with flavor.
Serving: 6-8
Preparation Time: 15 minutes
Ready Time: 1 hour

Ingredients:
- 1 pound ground beef
- 1 Tablespoon vegetable oil
- 1 onion, chopped
- 4 cloves garlic, minced
- 3/4 cup Guinness Stout
- 1 (16 ounce) can black beans, rinsed and drained
- 1 (15 ounce) can tomato sauce
- 1 teaspoon ground cumin
- 1 Tablespoon sugar
- 1/4 cup chopped fresh cilantro
- 12 (6 inch) corn or flour tortillas
- 2 cups shredded Mexican blend cheese
- Guacamole and Sour Cream for serving (optional)

Instructions:
1. Preheat oven to 350 degrees F (175 degrees C).
2. In a large skillet over medium heat, add the ground beef, oil, onion, and garlic. Cook and stir until the beef is evenly browned and cooked through, about 8 minutes.
3. Add the Guinness, black beans, tomato sauce, cumin, and sugar to the skillet. Simmer the mixture for 10 minutes.
4. Add the cilantro to the beef mixture and let cool slightly.
5. Spoon the beef mixture down the center of each tortilla, top with shredded cheese, and roll into a burrito. Place the burritos in a lightly greased 9x13 inch baking dish.
6. Bake in preheated oven for 20 minutes, or until cheese is melted.
7. Serve warm with guacamole and sour cream, if desired.

Nutrition information: Per serving: Calories: 435, Total Fat: 17g, Saturated Fat: 8g, Cholesterol: 58mg, Sodium: 564mg, Total Carbohydrates: 45g, Dietary Fiber: 7g, Protein: 22g.

77. Guinness Chocolate Pretzel Bites

Guinness Chocolate Pretzel Bites are a delicious way to enjoy the flavor of Guinness in a sweet and salty snack! They are easy to make and would make a great treat for any occasion.
Serving: 36 Bites
Preparation time: 15 minutes
Ready time: 25 minutes

Ingredients:
-1 package of pretzels
-1/2 cup Guinness
-1/2 cup sugar
-6 ounces semi-sweet chocolate chips
-2 Tablespoons butter

Instructions:
1. Preheat oven to 350°F.
2. Spread pretzels on a baking sheet.

3. In a small pot, mix together Guinness, sugar and butter. Heat on medium heat and stir occasionally until the sugar has dissolved.
4. Pour Guinness mixture over pretzels.
5. Bake in preheated oven for 15 minutes.
6. Remove from oven and let cool.
7. In a medium bowl, melt chocolate.
8. Using a spoon or a brush, coat each pretzel with the melted chocolate.
9. Place pretzels on parchment paper and let cool (or refrigerate).

Nutrition information: per 1 Bite (36 Bites): 45 cal, 0.8 g fat, 0 mg cholesterol, 79 mg sodium, 6.6 g carbohydrates, 0.4 g fiber, 5.4 g sugar, 2.2 g protein.

78. Guinness Braised Pork Tenderloin

Guinness Braised Pork Tenderloin is an incredibly flavorful, tender and easy to make meal that is sure to impress guests and family alike.
Serving: 4 servings
Preparation time: 15 minutes
Ready time: 2 hours

Ingredients:
-2 tablespoons olive oil
-2-3 pound pork tenderloin
-1 medium onion, thinly sliced
-3 cloves garlic, minced
-1 tablespoon tomato paste
-1 tablespoon minced fresh thyme
-1/2 teaspoon ground black pepper
-1 bay leaf
-1 ½ cups of Guinness beer
-1 tablespoon Worcestershire sauce
-1 tablespoon honey
-Kosher salt

Instructions:
1. Preheat oven to 350 degrees F.
2. Heat olive oil in a large oven-safe skillet over medium-high heat.

3. Season the pork tenderloin with Kosher salt and black pepper then add it to the skillet and cook it for 3 minutes per side.
4. Once the pork is browned, remove it from the pan and set aside on a plate.
5. Add the sliced onions and garlic to the skillet and cook, stirring frequently, for 3 minutes or until the onions are softened.
6. Add the tomato paste, thyme, bay leaf, Guinness, Worcestershire sauce and honey to the skillet and stir to combine.
7. Place the pork back into the skillet and spoon some of the Guinness mixture over the pork.
8. Place in the preheated oven and bake for 1 hour 15 minutes or until the pork reaches an internal temperature of 145 degrees F.
9. Once cooked, remove the pork to a plate and cover it with foil to keep it warm.
10. Strain the Guinness sauce over a fine-mesh strainer; discarding the solids in the strainer.
11. Simmer the strained liquid over low-medium heat for 10-15 minutes or until slightly reduced.
12. Slice the pork and serve with sauce spooned over it.

Nutrition information:
Calories – 375
Fat – 10.5g
Cholesterol – 143g
Carbohydrate – 8.3g
Protein – 50g
Sodium – 598mg

79. Guinness Chocolate Peanut Butter Bars

This easy-to-make sweet treat is sure to be a hit—Guinness Chocolate Peanut Butter Bars, made with just five simple Ingredients! The combination of Guinness-spiked peanut butter, cocoa powder, and melted Reese's pieces takes this bar cookie to new heights of deliciousness.
Serving: Makes 12 bars
Preparation time: 20 minutes
Ready time: 40 minutes

Ingredients:
- 6 tablespoons butter, melted
- ¾ cup creamy peanut butter
- ⅓ cup cocoa powder
- 2 tablespoons Guinness
- ½ cup Reese's pieces, melted

Instructions:
1. Preheat your oven to 375°F.
2. Line an 8-inch square baking pan with parchment paper.
3. In a bowl, combine the melted butter and peanut butter until smooth.
4. Next, add the cocoa powder and Guinness and stir again until combined.
5. Pour the mixture into the prepared baking pan.
6. Place pan in the oven and bake for 20 minutes, or until the edges starts to pull away from the sides of the pan.
7. Meanwhile, melt the Reese's pieces in a double boiler.
8. Remove the pan from the oven and pour the melted Reese's pieces on top.
9. Let cool before cutting into 12 bars.

Nutrition information
Per Serving: Calories 290; Total Fat 18g; Total Carbohydrate 24g; Protein 7g

80. Guinness Beer Brined Chicken

Enjoy a juicy chicken dish made with the flavors of a Guinness beer brine. This recipe is easy to prepare and requires just a few simple Ingredients.
Serving: 4
Preparation time: 10 minutes
Ready time: 4 hours

Ingredients:
-1 (12-ounce) can Guinness beer
-1 cup kosher salt

-1/2 cup light brown sugar
-1/4 cup molasses
-2 tablespoons black peppercorns
-2 tablespoons pickling spice
-4 quarts cold water
-2 chickens (about 3 1/2 pounds each)

Instructions:
1. In a large pot, combine the Guinness, salt, brown sugar, molasses, peppercorns, pickling spice, and water.
2. Bring the mixture to a boil, stirring occasionally. Once it has boiled, reduce the heat and let it simmer for 10 minutes.
3. Remove the pot from the heat and let the brine cool completely.
4. Place chickens in a large bowl and pour the cooled brine over them to cover. Cover the bowl with plastic wrap and place in the refrigerator for 4 hours.
5. Carefully remove the chickens from the brine and dry them off with paper towels.
6. Discard the brine and prepare the chickens for grilling or roasting according to your recipe.

Nutrition information: Calories: 425; Total Fat: 14g; Protein: 41g; Carbohydrates: 8g; Sodium: 353mg

81. Guinness Chocolate Hazelnut Tart

This Guinness Chocolate Hazelnut Tart combines two favorite flavors (Guinness and Chocolate) with the nutty, earthy flavor of toasted hazelnuts, creating a delicious and decadent tart.
Serving: Makes 8 servings
Preparation Time: 30 minutes
Ready Time: 1 hour

Ingredients:
-43/4 ounces bittersweet chocolate, chopped
-6 tablespoons butter
-1/3 cup plus 1 tablespoon all-purpose flour
-2 large eggs

-1/3 cup firmly packed dark brown sugar
-2 tablespoons defatted guinness*
-1/4 teaspoon salt
-3/4 cup lightly toasted hazelnuts

Instructions:
1. Preheat oven to 350 degrees F.
2. In a double boiler, over gently simmering water, melt the chocolate and butter, stirring until smooth. When the mixture is melted, remove from the heat and stir in the flour.
3. In a large bowl, combine the eggs, brown sugar, Guinness, and salt and beat with electric mixer on medium speed until blended.
4. Stir the chocolate mixture into the egg mixture. Stir in the hazelnuts.
5. Spoon the batter into a lightly greased 9" round tart pan. Bake for 40 to 45 minutes, or until a toothpick inserted in the center comes out clean. Let cool for 30 minutes before serving.

Nutrition information: Per Serving - Calories: 227 Total Fat: 16g Saturated Fat: 8g Cholesterol: 50mg Sodium: 111mg Total Carbohydrates: 19g Dietary Fiber: 1g Protein: 4g

82. Guinness Braised Veal Shanks

Guinness Braised Veal Shanks is a classic comfort food that covers all the bases with a deep and flavorful braising liquid made with Guinness beer. Succulent veal shanks are cooked low and slow until they are fall-off-the-bone tender.
Serving: 4
Preparation Time: 10 minutes
Ready Time: 2 hours 20 minutes

Ingredients:
• 2 tablespoons olive oil
• 2 veal shanks
• 2 carrots, roughly chopped
• 2 onions, roughly chopped
• 2 celery stalks, roughly chopped
• 2 cloves garlic, thinly sliced

- 2 tablespoons tomato paste
- 2 tablespoons fresh thyme leaves
- 2 bay leaves
- 2 tablespoons all-purpose flour
- 1 bottle Guinness beer
- 2 cups chicken stock
- Salt and freshly ground black pepper, to taste

Instructions:
1. Preheat oven to 350°F.
2. Heat oil in a large oven-safe skillet over medium heat.
3. Add veal shanks and brown on both sides, about 5 minutes.
4. Add carrots, onions, celery, and garlic and cook until softened, about 5 minutes.
5. Stir in tomato paste, thyme, and bay leaves.
6. Sprinkle flour over vegetables and stir to coat.
7. Pour in Guinness and chicken stock and season with salt and pepper.
8. Bring mixture to a simmer, then cover skillet and transfer to preheated oven.
9. Braise for 1 hour 30 minutes to 2 hours, or until meat is very tender.

Nutrition information: Per serving: Calories: 428, Fat: 24g, Carbohydrates: 14g, Protein: 38g, Sodium: 864mg, Fiber: 2g

83. Guinness Chocolate Raspberry Parfait

Guiness Chocolate Raspberry Parfait is a Bavarian-style dessert that blends together the sweet flavours of chocolate, raspberry and Guinness. This hearty yet delicious recipe is the ideal dessert for dinner parties or special occasions.
Serving: 4
Preparation Time: 25 minutes
Ready Time: 25 minutes

Ingredients:
- 1 – 6 pack of Guinness beer
- 4 ounces of semi-sweet chocolate chips
- 2 – 8 ounce containers of fresh raspberries

- 1 pint of heavy cream
- 1/4 cup of confectioners sugar

Instructions:
1. Preheat oven to 350°F.
2. Place beer in a medium-sized pot and heat over medium heat. Bring to a low simmer and add chocolate chips. Stir until melted.
3. In a separate bowl, mix together the raspberries and sugar.
4. In a blender or food processor, blend together the chocolate and beer mixture.
5. In a medium bowl, add the heavy cream and the raspberry mixture. Fold the mixture together until combined.
6. Divide the raspberry mixture among four 8-ounce glasses.
7. Gently pour the chocolate Guinness mixture over the raspberry mixture in each glass.
8. Bake in the preheated oven for 15 minutes.
9. Serve warm.

Nutrition information: Calories: 310 Kcal, Fat: 19 g, Carbohydrates: 27 g, Protein: 5 g, Sodium: 89 mg

84. Guinness Beef Quesadillas

Savory and delicious, Guinness Beef Quesadillas are a hearty and flavorful Mexican-style dish that comes together quickly. Serve with salsa, sour cream, or guacamole for the perfect snacking experience.
Serving: 4
Preparation Time: 10 minutes
Ready Time: 15 minutes

Ingredients:
- 1 lb ground beef
- 4 tablespoons Guinness beer
- 2 teaspoons chili flakes
- 1 teaspoon ground cumin
- 1 teaspoon smoked paprika
- Salt, to taste
- 8 small flour tortillas

- 1 cup shredded Mexican cheese blend

Instructions:
1. Preheat a large skillet over medium heat and add the ground beef. Cook, breaking up with a wooden spoon, until browned.
2. Add the beer and spices and cook for a further 2 minutes. Season with salt to taste.
3. Place a flour tortilla in the heated skillet and sprinkle some shredded cheese over it.
4. Top with some of the Guinness beef and sprinkle more cheese on top. Place another tortilla on top and press lightly.
5. Cook for 2 minutes before flipping and cooking for a further 2 minutes.
6. Divide the quesadilla into 4 pieces and serve with your favourite toppings.

Nutrition information:
Calories: 375, Total Fat: 17g, Cholesterol: 58mg, Sodium: 279mg, Total Carbohydrates: 25g, Protein: 24g

85. Guinness Chocolate Coconut Macaroons

Delicious Guinness Chocolate Coconut Macaroons are a favorite holiday treat! Made with rich cocoa and creamy coconut, they are perfect for sharing with friends and family.
Serving: Makes about 24 macaroons
Preparation Time: 10 minutes
Ready Time: 30 minutes

Ingredients:
• 2 cups shredded coconut
• 2/3 cup sweetened condensed milk
• 2 tablespoons Guinness stout beer
• 2 tablespoons cocoa powder
• 1 teaspoon vanilla extract
• 2 tablespoons flour
• 1/2 teaspoon salt

Instructions:
1. Preheat the oven to 350°F. Line a baking sheet with parchment paper.
2. In a medium bowl, combine the coconut, condensed milk, Guinness, cocoa powder, vanilla extract, flour, and salt.
3. Mix everything together until a thick dough is formed.
4. Scoop the dough onto the prepared baking sheet, forming small mounds that are about 2 inches in diameter.
5. Bake for 15-20 minutes, until golden brown.
6. Cool before serving.

Nutrition information:
• Calories: 100• Protein: 2 g • Fat: 7 g • Carbohydrates: 7 g• Sodium: 65 mg• Fiber: 1 g

86. Guinness Braised Salmon

Guinness Braised Salmon is an easy and healthy one-dish meal to prepare. The Guinness beer and soy sauce provides a unique and delicious flavor while the salmon is tender and savory.
Serving: 4
Preparation time: 10 minutes
Ready time: 30 minutes

Ingredients:
• 4 salmon filets
• 1 cup of Guinness beer
• 2 cloves of garlic, minced
• 1/4 cup of soy sauce
• 2 tablespoons of honey
• 2 tablespoons of olive oil

Instructions:
1. Preheat oven to 375°F
2. Heat olive oil in a large oven safe skillet over medium heat.
3. Add garlic and sauté for 1 minute.
4. Add salmon filets to pan and cook for 2 minutes per side.
5. Add Guinness, soy sauce and honey to pan.
6. Bring to a simmer and cook for 2-3 minutes.

7. Transfer skillet to the oven and bake for 8-10 minutes.
8. Serve the salmon with the pan sauce.

Nutrition information:
• Calories: 342
• Total fat: 16.1g
• Saturated fat: 2.7g
• Protein: 39.2g
• Sodium: 663mg
• Carbohydrates: 9.3g
• Fiber: 0.2g

87. Guinness Chocolate Cherry Cake

Guinness Chocolate Cherry Cake is a delicious dessert perfect for any occasion, combining two much-loved flavors of Guinness beer and chocolate!
Serving: 8
Preparation Time: 15 minutes
Ready Time: 50 minutes

Ingredients:
• 2/3 cup Guinness stout
• 1 stick butter
• 3/4 cup cocoa powder
• 2 eggs
• 1 1/2 cups of all-purpose flour
• 1/4 teaspoon salt
• 2/3 cup sour cream
• 3/4 cup sugar
• 1 teaspoon baking soda
• 1/2 cup glacé cherries, chopped
• 1/2 cup semi-sweet chocolate chips

Instructions:
1. Preheat the oven to 350°F. Grease and flour an 8" round cake pan.
2. In a saucepan, combine Guinness, butter and cocoa powder and heat until everything is melted and combined.

3. In a separate bowl, mix together the eggs, flour, salt, sour cream, sugar and baking soda.
4. Slowly stir in the Guinness mixture and mix completely.
5. Stir in cherries and chocolate chips.
6. Pour the batter into the prepared cake pan and bake for 40-45 minutes, or until a toothpick inserted into the center of the cake comes out clean.
7. Let the cake cool for 10 minutes, then turn out onto a wire rack to cool completely.

Nutrition information: Per Serving – 322 calories; Fat 11.6g; Carbohydrates 47.3g; Cholesterol 56.7mg; Sodium 293.3mg; Protein 4.1g.

88. Guinness Beef Nachos

Guinness Beef Nachos are the perfect indulgence for game day or any day those nacho cravings strike! A combination of seasoned beef, crispy chips, and melted cheese, these nachos are sure to be a hit.
Serving: 6
Preparation Time: 10 minutes
Ready Time: 30 minutes

Ingredients:
-1 lb lean ground beef
-1 tablespoon olive oil
-1/2 cup diced onion
-2 cloves garlic, minced
-2 tablespoons chili powder
-1 teaspoon salt
-1/2 teaspoon ground cumin
-1/2 teaspoon dried oregano
-1/4 teaspoon ground black pepper
-1/4 teaspoon cayenne pepper
-1 cup Guinness Beer
-1 can (14.5 oz) diced tomatoes
-1 can (4 oz) diced green chiles
-8 ounces tortilla chips

-1.5 cups shredded Mexican cheese blend
-Sour cream and green onions for serving

Instructions:
1. Preheat the oven to 375°F.
2. Heat the olive oil in a large skillet over medium-high heat. Add the ground beef and cook until browned. Drain the fat, then add the onion, garlic, chili powder, salt, cumin, oregano, black pepper, and cayenne pepper to the pan. Cook for an additional 3 minutes, then stir in the Guinness beer and diced tomatoes. Simmer for 15 minutes.
3. Spread the chips out on a baking sheet. Top with the beef mixture, and sprinkle the cheese over the top.
4. Bake in the preheated oven for 15 minutes, or until the cheese is melted and bubbly.
5. Serve warm with sour cream, green onions, and your favorite nacho toppings.

Nutrition information: Calories 425, Fat 21 g, Saturated Fat 8 g, Carbohydrates 27 g, Fiber 4 g, Protein 25 g, Sodium 720 mg

89. Guinness Chocolate Caramel Macchiato

This delicious Guinness Chocolate Caramel Macchiato is the perfect indulgent beverage. The combination of robust espresso, decadent chocolate, and sweet caramel make this a heavenly coffee drink.
Serving:
This recipe makes 2 macchiatos.
Preparation time: 10 minutes
Ready time: 6 minutes

Ingredients:
- 2 shots of espresso
- 2 tablespoons of caramel syrup
- 2 tablespoons of chocolate syrup
- 1/2 cup of Guinness Stout
- 2 cups of steamed milk

Instructions:

1. Pull the espresso shots and add them to a cup.
2. Add the caramel and chocolate syrup and stir.
3. Pour the Guinness into the cup and stir again.
4. Heat the milk in a pan and add it to the espresso mixture.
5. Top off the mixture with foam and enjoy!

Nutrition information:
Per serving: 298 Kcal, 29 g carbohydrates, 11 g fat, 2 g protein

90. Guinness Braised Duck Breast

Guinness Braised Duck Breasts are sure to please any dinner guest. The succulent poultry is cooked in a delicious and flavorful Guinness Beer-based sauce that's sure to have you coming back for more.
Serving: Makes four servings.
Preparation time: 10 minutes
Ready time: 2 hours

Ingredients:
• 4 duck breasts
• 3 cloves garlic
• 1 large onion, chopped
• 2 cups Guinness beer
• 2 tablespoons olive oil
• 2 tablespoons butter
• 1 sprig fresh thyme
• 1 tablespoon dijon mustard
• 2 tablespoons maple syrup

Instructions:
1. Preheat oven to 375 degrees Fahrenheit.
2. Heat olive oil and butter in an oven-safe skillet over medium-high heat. Add garlic and onions, cooking until softened.
3. Add duck breasts to the skillet and cook until lightly browned, about 5 minutes per side.
4. Pour Guinness beer into the skillet and add thyme and dijon mustard. Bring to a boil, reduce heat, and simmer for 5 minutes.

5. Add the maple syrup and simmer for an additional 5 minutes before transferring the skillet to the preheated oven.
6. Bake in the oven for 25-30 minutes or until cooked through.
7. Remove from oven, slice duck breasts, and serve atop the Guinness sauce.

Nutrition information: Per serving: 330 calories, 20g fat, 9g carbohydrates, 22g protein.

91. Guinness Chocolate Banana Bread

Introducing Guinness Chocolate Banana Bread—a unique twist on the classic favorite that adds a smoky-sweet factor thanks to a hint of beer. Serving: Makes one 9-inch loaf Preparation time: 10 minutes Ready time: 2 hours

Ingredients:
1 ½ cups all-purpose flour
1 teaspoon baking soda
½ teaspoon salt
2 tablespoons unsalted butter, melted
1 cup mashed ripe banana (approximately 2 bananas)
¼ cup Guinness Extra Stout beer
½ cup sugar
2 eggs
½ cup chopped semisweet chocolate

Instructions:
 Preheat the oven to 350°F and lightly grease a 9-inch loaf pan with butter.
In a medium bowl, whisk together the flour, baking soda and salt.
In a large bowl, whisk together the melted butter, banana, Guinness, sugar and eggs. Using a wooden spoon, mix in the flour mixture until just combined. Gently fold in the chopped chocolate.
Pour the batter into the prepared loaf pan and bake for 45 to 55 minutes, until the top is golden brown and a toothpick inserted into the center comes out clean.
Let the loaf cool before slicing and serving.

Nutrition information: Serving Size: 1 slice • Calories: 235 • Fat: 7g • Carbs: 38g • Protein: 4g • Sodium: 207mg • Sugar: 19g

92. Guinness BBQ Pork Sliders

Enjoy these sweet and savory Guinness BBQ Pork Sliders, which are made in your slow cooker with a secret sauce that has beer included! Serve with your favorite potato side dish and you'll have an easy meal the whole family will love.

Serving: Makes 8 sliders
Preparation Time: 10 minutes
Ready Time: 4 hours 15 minutes

Ingredients:
• 2 lbs. boneless pork shoulder roast
• 1 cup lager beer (such as Guinness)
• ½ cup tomato-based chili sauce
• 4 tsp. Worcestershire sauce
• 2 tsp. garlic powder
• 2 cloves garlic, minced
• 1 medium onion, diced
• 8 mini slider buns

Instructions:
1. Cut the pork shoulder into cubes about 1 inch each.
2. Place the cubes into a 6-quart slow cooker.
3. In a small bowl, combine the beer, chili sauce, Worcestershire sauce, garlic powder, garlic and onion.
4. Pour the sauce over the pork cubes in the slow cooker.
5. Cover the slow cooker and cook on low for 4 hours or until pork is tender.
6. Shred the pork with two forks.
7. Place the pork onto the slider buns and serve.

Nutrition information: Calories: 259, Fat: 11.5g, Carbohydrates: 8g, Protein: 20g, Sodium: 257mg, Fiber: 1g

93. Guinness Chocolate Creme Brulee

Indulge in a delicious, creamy Guinness Chocolate Creme Brulee that blends sweet and creamy custard with the unique flavor of Guinness.
Serving: Makes 6 servings.
Preparation Time: 10 minutes
Ready Time: 8 hours

Ingredients:
• 2 (12 ounces) bottles Guinness Draught
• 1 cup heavy whipping cream
• 1/2 cup sugar
• 2 tablespoons cornstarch
• 4 eggs
• 3 ounces dark chocolate, chopped
• 1 teaspoon vanilla extract

Instructions:
1. Preheat oven to 325°F.
2. In a medium saucepan, heat Guinness and heavy whipping cream over medium-high heat until mixture boils. Reduce heat and allow to simmer for 10 minutes.
3. In a separate bowl, whisk together sugar and cornstarch. Add eggs and continue whisking until the mixture is thick.
4. Reduce heat to low and slowly pour in the egg mixture, whisking constantly. Cook for an additional 3 minutes, stirring constantly.
5. Take the saucepan off the heat. Stir in the chopped dark chocolate and vanilla extract.
6. Divide the mixture among 6 (6-ounce) ramekins. Place ramekins in a baking dish and fill with water until it's about halfway up the sides of the ramekins.
7. Bake in preheated oven for 25 to 30 minutes, or until custards are lightly golden and fully set.
8. Let custards cool to room temperature, then chill in the refrigerator for at least 8 hours or overnight.

Nutrition information:
• Calories: 287

- Total Fat: 17g
- Saturated Fat: 10g
- Trans Fat: 0g
- Cholesterol: 135mg
- Sodium: 79mg
- Carbohydrates: 25g
- Fiber: 1g
- Sugar: 18g
- Protein: 6g

94. Guinness Braised Rabbit Stew

This Guinness Braised Rabbit Stew is an easy, savory, and comforting meal that's full of flavor. The hearty stew is a cozy dish that's cooked in a flavorful Guinness broth with carrots, celery, and potatoes.
Serving: 6
Preparation time: 10 minutes
Ready time: 1 hour and 15 minutes

Ingredients:
- 2 tablespoons olive oil
- 2-3 pounds rabbit, cut into 8 pieces
- 2 onions, chopped
- 2 carrots, peeled and diced
- 2 stalks celery, diced
- 2 cloves garlic, minced
- 2 tablespoons dried thyme
- 2 tablespoons flour
- 2 500ml bottles of Guinness beer
- 2 cups chicken stock
- 1 pound potatoes, cut into chunks
- 2 tablespoons chopped fresh parsley
- 2 tablespoons chopped fresh chives

Instructions:
1. Heat the oil in a large Dutch oven over medium-high heat. Add in the rabbit pieces and fry 2-3 minutes per side. Transfer to a plate.
2. Add the onions and fry until softened, about 5 minutes.

3. Add the carrots, celery, and garlic and cook for 2 minutes.
4. Sprinkle with the thyme and flour and stir to combine.
5. Pour in the Guinness and chicken stock, and add the rabbit pieces back to the pot.
6. Bring to a boil, reduce the heat to low, and simmer for 45 minutes.
7. Add the potatoes, cover, and cook for an additional 30 minutes.
8. Add the parsley and chives, and season with salt and pepper to taste.
Nutrition: Calories: 621, Carbohydrates: 37 g, Protein: 37 g, Fat: 25 g, Saturated Fat: 4 g, Cholesterol: 109 mg, Sodium: 556 mg, Fiber: 4 g, Sugar: 9 g

95. Guinness Chocolate Mint Cookies

Guinness Chocolate Mint Cookies are an incredible combination of flavors. They are crunchy on the outside, chewy on the inside, and of course, packed with intense chocolaty-minty goodness.
Serving: Makes 24 cookies
Preparation time: 10 minutes
Ready time: 20 minutes

Ingredients:
- 2 cups all-purpose flour
- 1/2 teaspoon baking powder
- 1/2 teaspoon baking soda
- 1/2 teaspoon salt
- 1/2 cup (1 stick) unsalted butter, softened
- 1 cup packed brown sugar
- 1/2 cup granulated sugar
- 1 large egg
- 1 teaspoon pure vanilla extract
- 1 teaspoon peppermint extract
- 1 (12-ounce) package semi-sweet chocolate chips
- 2 tablespoons Guinness Stout

Instructions:
1. Preheat oven to 350 degrees F.
2. In a medium bowl, whisk together flour, baking powder, baking soda, and salt; set aside.

3. In the bowl of an electric mixer fitted with the paddle attachment, beat butter, sugars, egg, vanilla, and peppermint until light and fluffy.

4. With the mixer running on low speed, gradually add flour mixture and beat until just combined.

5. In a medium bowl, combine chocolate chips and Guinness. Stir until melted and combined.

6. Gradually add chocolate mixture to the butter mixture and beat until just combined.

7. Line baking sheets with parchment paper and scoop dough onto prepared baking sheets. Bake for 8-10 minutes or until edges are just golden.

8. Allow cookies to cool slightly before transferring to a wire rack to cool completely.

Nutrition information: Serving Size: 1 cookie, Calories: 145, Fat: 5.5g, Cholesterol: 18mg, Sodium: 96mg, Carbohydrates: 22g, Protein: 1g.

96. Guinness Beef Fajitas

Guinness Beef Fajitas are an Irish twist on the Mexican favorite. These fajitas made with flavorful, tender beef, peppers, onions, and fragrant Guinness beer are sure to be a crowd pleaser!

Serving: 4
Preparation Time: 10 minutes
Ready Time: 40 minutes

Ingredients:
- 1 ½ lbs. sirloin steak
- 2 tablespoons of olive oil
- ¼ cup of Guinness beer
- 2 bell peppers, thinly sliced
- 1 onion, thinly sliced
- 2 cloves of garlic, minced
- 2 tablespoons of taco seasoning
- Salt and pepper
- Tortillas, for Serving:

Instructions:
1. Heat the olive oil in a large skillet over medium high heat.
2. In a bowl, combine the steak strips, Guinness, garlic, and taco seasoning.
3. Add the steak mixture to the skillet and cook for 8-10 minutes, stirring occasionally, until the steak is cooked through.
4. Add the bell peppers and onions and cook for an additional 5 minutes, or until the peppers and onions are tender.
5. Serve the steak and vegetables in tortillas with your desired toppings.

Nutrition information: Calories: 409; Fat: 17g; Carbs: 27g; Protein: 36g

97. Guinness Chocolate Toffee Bars

Guinness Chocolate Toffee Bars are a decadent dessert that combine rich Guinness beer and toffee and are topped with lots of chocolate.
Serving: 16 bars
Preparation Time: 20 minutes
Ready Time: 1 hour

Ingredients:
• 1 (14.9-ounce) bottle Guinness Draught
• 1/2 cup (1 stick) butter
• 1/4 cup firmly packed light brown sugar
• 9 graham cracker rectangles, broken into pieces
• 1/2 cup chopped toffee candy bars
• 2 1/2 cups semisweet chocolate chips
• 1/4 teaspoon sea salt
• 1 teaspoon vanilla extract

Instructions:
1. Preheat oven to 350 degrees F. Spray an 8x8-inch baking pan with non stick cooking spray.
2. In a medium saucepan, heat butter over low heat until melted. Add the Guinness Draught and stir until combined. Whisk in the brown sugar and cook for about 5 minutes over medium-low heat.

3. Place the graham cracker pieces into a medium bowl. Pour the Guinness mixture over the top and stir until fully combined. Pour the mixture into prepared pan. Bake for 12-15 minutes.

4. Place the toffee pieces into a small bowl and set aside.

5. In a medium saucepan over low heat, stir together the chocolate chips, sea salt, and vanilla extract until melted and smooth.

6. Spread the melted chocolate over the toffee bars. Sprinkle with toffee pieces and lightly press down. Place in the refrigerator until set, about 30 minutes.

Nutrition information: Serving Size: 1 bar, Calories: 210, Fat: 10g, Cholesterol: 10mg, Sodium: 140mg, Carbohydrates: 28g, Protein: 2g

98. Guinness Braised Lamb Chops

This delicious dish is a great way to enjoy high-quality lamb chops, carefully cooked in Guinness beer. The rich flavors of the beer make the chops so juicy and full of flavor!

Serving: 4

Preparation time: 15 minutes

Ready time: 1 hour

Ingredients:
- 4 lamb chops
- 2 tablespoons of olive oil
- 1 cup Guinness beer
- 2 cloves of garlic, crushed
- ½ cup chopped fresh rosemary
- Salt and pepper to taste

Instructions:
1. Preheat your oven to 350 F.

2. Place the olive oil in a large skillet over medium-high heat, and when it's hot, add the lamb chops. Sear them on both sides, about 2 minutes per side.

3. Remove the lamb chops from the skillet and set aside.

4. Pour the Guinness beer into the skillet and add the garlic, rosemary, salt, and pepper. Bring the mixture to a boil.

5. Reduce the heat to low and add the lamb chops back to the skillet.
6. Place the skillet in the preheated oven and cook for 40 minutes.
7. Remove the skillet from the oven and serve the lamb chops hot.

Nutrition information:
Calories: 281 kcal
Total Fat: 13.2g
Saturated Fat: 3.3g
Cholesterol: 61mg
Sodium: 64mg
Carbohydrates: 1.9g
Protein: 33.9g

99. Guinness Chocolate Almond Biscotti

Guinness Chocolate Almond Biscotti is the perfect crunchy biscuit to accompany your afternoon tea or coffee. Making them at home is easy and the recipe makes a delightful gift for family and friends.
Serving: Makes about 15-17 biscotti
Preparation Time: 15 minutes
Ready Time: 25 minutes

Ingredients:
- 140 g all-purpose flour
- 60 g cocoa powder
- 150 g sugar
- 1 tablespoon baking powder
- 1 pinch salt
- 2 tablespoons instant espresso powder
- 2 tablespoons Guinness beer
- 2 teaspoons almond extract
- 120 g slivered almonds
- 40 g semisweet chocolate chips

Instructions:
• Preheat oven to 350 degrees F (175 degrees C).

- In a medium bowl, stir together the flour, cocoa powder, sugar, baking powder, salt, espresso powder, Guinness beer and almond extract until thoroughly blended.
- Work in the slivered almonds and chocolate chips until evenly distributed throughout the dough.
- Divide the dough into two pieces, and shape each piece into a log about 8 inches long.
- Place logs on a lightly greased baking sheet and bake for 15 minutes. Remove from oven and let cool.
- Cut the logs into slices about 1/4 to 1/2 inch thick.
- Place slices on lightly greased baking sheet and return to oven and bake for 10 minutes, or until slightly firm.

Nutrition information: (per 1 Biscotti):
- Calories: 115
- Fat: 4.6 g
- Carbohydrates: 15.6 g
- Protein: 2.2 g
- Fiber: 1.1 g

100. Guinness Stout Ice Cream

This creamy Guinness Stout Ice Cream recipe is the perfect balance of sweet and bitter. Rich, creamy, and bursting with flavor, this no-churn ice cream is sure to become a favorite.
Serving: 6-8
Preparation Time: 5 minutes
Ready Time: 4 hours

Ingredients:
2 cups heavy cream
2/3 cup granulated sugar
1 cup Guinness Stout beer
1 teaspoon vanilla extract

Instructions:
1. Using an electric mixer, beat cream and sugar on medium to high speed until the sugar is dissolved and the cream holds its shape.

2. Reduce the speed to low and slowly pour in the Guinness Stout beer. Mix until combined then add in the vanilla extract.
3. Pour the mixture into a freezer safe container and freeze for 4 hours. If using a traditional ice cream machine, follow the manufacturer's instructions.

Nutrition information:
Calories: 138 kcal ; Carbohydrates: 7 g ; Protein: 0 g ; Fat: 11 g ; Sodium: 10 mg ; Potassium: 29 mg ; Sugar: 6 g.

101. Guinness Chocolate Caramel Trifle

Guinness Chocolate Caramel Trifle is a creamy, delicious dessert with layers of chocolate cake, dark beer, caramel, and white chocolate mousse. It's the perfect indulgent treat to enjoy after a great meal.
Serving: 8-10
Preparation Time: 45 minutes
Ready Time: 6 hours

Ingredients:
- 1 package of chocolate cake mix, plus Ingredients listed on box
- 1 bottle dark Irish stout beer (like Guinness)
- 1/2 cup of caramel sauce
- 1/2 bag semi-sweet or dark chocolate chips
- 1 quart heavy cream
- 2/3 cup white chocolate chips
- 1/4 cup confectioners' sugar
- 1/2 teaspoon almond extract

Instructions:
1. Preheat oven to 350 F. Prepare and bake cake mix according to directions. Let cool.
2. In a bowl, combine 1 bottle of Guinness and 1/2 cup of caramel sauce and mix until fully combined. Set aside.
3. Add semi-sweet or dark chocolate chips and white chocolate chips to the Guinness and caramel sauce mixture and stir until all chips are combined.

4. Whip heavy cream, confectioners' sugar, and almond extract together until the cream is light and fluffy.
5. Cut the cooled cake into 1-inch cubes.
6. In a trifle bowl, begin layering the mousse, cake cubes, and Guinness-chocolate-caramel mixture. Repeat until all Ingredients are used. Place in the refrigerator and chill for 6 hours or overnight.

Nutrition information:
Calories: 500, Protein: 8g, Fat: 27g, Carbs: 58g, Fiber: 2g, Sugars: 33g, Sodium: 300mg, Cholesterol: 70mg

102. Guinness Braised Chicken Wings

Guinness Braised Chicken Wings are an easy and savory recipe that yields perfectly cooked wings that are full of flavor.
Serving: 4
Preparation Time: 5 minutes
Ready Time: 45 minutes

Ingredients:
• 2 lbs chicken wings
• 1/2 cup dark Guinness beer
• 2 tablespoons Worcestershire sauce
• 2 cloves garlic, minced
• 2 tablespoons brown sugar
• 2 tablespoons butter
• 1 teaspoon salt

Instructions:
1. Preheat the oven to 375F.
2. In a bowl, mix together Guinness beer, Worcestershire sauce, garlic, brown sugar, butter and salt.
3. Place the chicken wings in a baking dish. Pour the mixture over the wings, and ensure all the wings are evenly coated.
4. Bake the wings in the preheated oven for 40-45 minutes or until the chicken is cooked through and golden.
5. Let the chicken cool for 5 minutes before serving.

Nutrition information: Calories: 392, Carbohydrates: 11 g, Protein: 30 g, Fat: 22 g, Saturated Fat: 7 g, Cholesterol: 111 mg, Sodium: 968 mg, Potassium: 218 mg, Sugar: 8 g, Vitamin A: 126 IU, Vitamin C: 1 mg, Calcium: 14 mg, Iron: 1 mg.

103. Guinness Chocolate Stout Cake

This Guinness Chocolate Stout Cake is a deliciously moist cake that is a chocolate lovers dream with a hint of stout. It's the perfect treat for your next party!
Serving: 10-12
Preparation time: 20-25 minutes
Ready time: 65 minutes

Ingredients:
-1 cup Guinness stout beer
-2 cups all purpose flour
-2/3 cup Dutch-processed cocoa powder
-1 teaspoon baking soda
-1 teaspoon salt
-1 cup unsalted butter, at room temperature
-2 cups granulated sugar
-4 large eggs
-1/2 cup sour cream

Instructions:
1. Preheat the oven to 350F. Grease a 9-inch spring form pan with butter.
2. In a medium bowl, whisk together the flour, cocoa powder, baking soda, and salt. Set aside.
3. In the bowl of an electric mixer, beat the butter and sugar together until light and fluffy.
4. Add the eggs one at a time, mixing until fully incorporated.
5. Add the sour cream and Guinness and mix until combined.
6. Slowly add the dry Ingredients and mix until just combined.
7. Pour the batter into the prepared pan and bake for 50-60 minutes, or until a toothpick inserted into the center of the cake comes out clean.

8. Let cool in the pan for 10-15 minutes before transferring to a wire rack to cool completely.

Nutrition information:
Calories: 305, Total Fat: 11.8g, Cholesterol: 69mg, Sodium: 437mg, Carbohydrates: 42.4g, Protein: 4.5g, Fiber: 2.2g

104. Guinness Beef and Guinness Pie

Guinness Beef and Guinness Pie is an easy and hearty dinner dish that features flavorful beef, potatoes, and Guinness beer. This British-style dish is great for a family dinner, or can be served as part of a St. Patrick's Day celebration.
Serving: 4
Preparation Time: 15 minutes
Ready Time: 1 hour and 5 minutes

Ingredients:
- 2 tablespoons olive oil
- 1 large onion, chopped
- 1 lb beef chuck roast, cubed
- 2 cloves garlic, minced
- 1 teaspoon sea salt
- 1/2 teaspoon cracked pepper
- 1/4 teaspoon smoked paprika
- 1/4 teaspoon cumin
- 1 cup beef broth
- 1 (12 oz) can Guinness Extra Stout beer
- 2 tablespoons tomato paste
- 1 teaspoon Worcestershire sauce
- 2 tablespoons all-purpose flour
- 2 large potatoes, peeled and chopped
- 1/2 cup frozen peas
- 1/2 cup frozen corn
- 1/2 cup shredded cheddar cheese
- 1 unbaked pie crust

Instructions:

1. Preheat oven to 350°F.
2. In a large skillet over medium-high heat, heat oil. Add onion and cook until softened, about 3 minutes.
3. Add beef cubes, garlic, salt, pepper, paprika, and cumin. Cook until beef is browned, about 8 minutes.
4. Add beef broth, Guinness, tomato paste, and Worcestershire sauce. Simmer for 15 minutes.
5. In a small bowl, whisk together flour and some of the liquids from the beef mixture. Stir the flour mixture into the skillet and mix until combined.
6. Stir in potatoes, peas, and corn. Cook for 5 minutes.
7. Grease a 9 inch pie plate. Place the beef mixture into the pie plate. Sprinkle the cheese on top.
8. Place the pie crust over the beef mixture and crimp the edges. Cut slits into the crust to allow steam to escape.
9. Bake for 35-40 minutes, or until crust is golden and filling is bubbly.

Nutrition information: Per Serving: 360 calories, 15g fat, 29g carbohydrates, 17g protein

105. Guinness Chocolate Coconut Cream Pie

Guinness Chocolate Coconut Cream Pie is a delicious and unique combination of flavors giving you a sweet and savory dessert.
Serving: Serves 8-10.
Preparation Time: 25 minutes
Ready Time: 2 hours

Ingredients:
• 2 cups graham cracker crumbs
• 1/3 cup white sugar
• 5 tablespoons melted butter
• 1 (14 ounce) can sweetened condensed milk
• 3/4 cup Guinness stout
• 1/2 cup semisweet chocolate chips
• 2 tablespoons butter
• 3/4 cup toasted coconut
• 1/2 teaspoon vanilla extract

• 2 eggs beaten
• 1 (8 ounce) container frozen whipped topping, thawed

Instructions:
1. Preheat oven to 350 degrees F (175 degrees C).
2. In a bowl, mix the graham cracker crumbs, sugar, and melted butter. Press this mixture into the bottom and sides of a 9-inch pie pan. Bake at 350 degrees F (175 degrees C) for 8 minutes.
3. In a saucepan, combine the condensed milk, Guinness, chocolate chips, and 2 tablespoons butter. Cook over medium heat until thickened, stirring constantly. Remove the mixture from the heat and stir in the coconut and vanilla. Let cool slightly.
4. Beat the eggs in a bowl and slowly add in the warm chocolate mixture, stirring constantly. Pour the mixture into the prepared pie crust. Bake at 350 degrees F (175 degrees C) for 35 minutes. Cool until room temperature.
5. Frost the pie with whipped topping and refrigerate for at least 2 hours before serving.

Nutrition information: Nutrition information per serving: 213 calories; 8.6 g fat; 0.6 g saturated fat; 27 mg cholesterol; 90 mg sodium; 27.7 g carbohydrates; 1.8 g fiber; 18 g sugar; 4 g protein.

CONCLUSION

The "Pour Me Another: 105 Guinness Recipes" cookbook is a fantastic resource for learning about unique stouts, ales, and porters from around the world. The mix of classic and easy to prepare recipes make it the perfect book for any Guinness lover and aspiring home brewer. With tips from seasoned pros and detailed explanations for novices alike, the reader is sure to gain a better understanding and appreciation for this iconic beer. From simple snacks and appetizers to full-course dinners, this cookbook offers recipes for every occasion. Whether you're looking to enjoy a pint with friends, pair an exceptional meal with the perfect beer, or simply want to treat yourself to some delicious Guinness-infused recipes, this cookbook provides a truly unique culinary experience. With over one hundred recipes to choose from, this cookbook serves as a great introduction to the wonderful world of Guinness, allowing you to explore its variety and depth of flavors. From Crispy Guinness Fish Fingers to Banana and Guinness Ice Cream, the breadth of recipes available covers the entirety of the Guinness family. Moreover, this cookbook is a great way to learn about cooking and baking with beer, from basic preparation techniques to more advanced methods. Whether you're looking to elevate your culinary repertoire or just want to explore the unique flavors of Guinness, the "Pour Me Another: 105 Guinness Recipes" cookbook is the perfect place to start. Experienced brewers and novices alike are sure to find something to enjoy in this wonderful cookbook.

Printed in Dunstable, United Kingdom